SECOND THOUGHTS

One Hundred Upbeat Messages for Beat-Up Americans

Mort Crim

television anchor, radio broadcaster and
creator of the internationally syndicated
series *Second Thoughts*

D0103647

Health Communications, Inc.
Deerfield Beach, Florida

www.hci-online.com

Library of Congress Cataloging-in-Publication Data

Cataloging-in-Publication data is available from the Library of Congress.

©1997 Mort Crim Communications, Inc.

ISBN 1-55874-566-1

Publisher: Health Communications, Inc.
          3201 S.W. 15th Street
          Deerfield Beach, FL 33442-8190

Cover design by Lawna P. Oldfield
Cover photos courtesy of Mort Crim Communications, Inc.

To my wife,
Renee,
whose love and cheerfulness
keep me *upbeat.*

And to my children,
Albert and Carey,
who bring me joy today and
hope for tomorrow.

Contents

Foreword

When Mort Crim asked me to write the foreword to his book, he couldn't have picked a more inappropriate person. You see, I don't do well with people who come up to me in the middle of my latest personal crisis and tell me that "behind every cloud there's a silver lining." I say, "Show me a cloud with a lining, silver or otherwise, and I'll buy Ohio." I am also a firm believer that there's no point in "looking at the bright side" because in my mental house when the lights go out, it gets dark. Very dark. Every time something goes horribly wrong and I'm told this experience will make me "appreciate life all the more," I reply, "No, it won't. It will only reinforce the cynical view I already have."

But Mort was persistent, and since I have trouble saying no, I decided to give it a shot. Maybe I'd learn something, right? Maybe pick up a tip or two? What could it hurt?

Well, the truth is, it made me think. Differently.

According to Mort, there is good in the world if we take the time to find it. He believes there's such a thing as the power of positive thought and if we make the effort to exercise that part of our brain, we can change ourselves and others. Maybe even the world we live in. All this from a guy who spent 30 years reporting blood and gore every night on the 11:00 news.

Hey, if he can do it . . .

Jeff Daniels

Acknowledgments

Every person who has ever touched my life has contributed to this book. A few deserve special mention:

My wife, Renee, for your patience and support during long days of scriptwriting, and for ideas, suggestions and honest opinions; most of all, for your enduring love.

My children, Albert and Carey, for your candid critiques, your belief in me and your enthusiasm for my work. You know how to humble me and honor me, and I love you both dearly.

My stepsons, Jeffrey and Randy Miller, and Randy's wife, Jamie. No one could ask for a nicer extended family or for more delightful grandchildren than Zachery and Emily.

My mother, Ocie, and my father, Albert, whose positive influence and daily examples of faith shaped my sense of optimism and instilled a sense of personal responsibility.

My uncle Alvah Crim and my aunt Vera Martin, both gifted with an outrageous sense of humor that belied their dedication as minister and medical missionary. They taught me to take my *work* seriously but not *myself.*

My late wife, Nicki, whose faith, optimism and love for her family remained strong until the end. She would not be surprised by the success of the *Second Thoughts* radio series. Nicki always expected the best.

Nicki's brother Chuck Dale, my in-law by circumstance but my good friend and business associate by choice. Chuck and his wife, Sandy, graciously opened their home for the very first focus group to determine whether *Second Thoughts* had any future on the radio.

Joe Antonini, for your faith in me and in the message of *Second Thoughts.* You made everything possible—the radio feature and the book—and I'll always be grateful.

Tom Clark, good friend, advisor and advertising guru. (I would have said *genius,* but you're so humble, Tom, I didn't want to embarrass you.)

Paul Harvey, for friendship, for inspiration and for teaching all of us how to say much with few words.

The Reverend R. Eugene Sterner, friend, mentor and expert in the art of living.

Cindy Carney, Silvia Fiondo and Lisa Hubbs, my three secretaries and strong right arms (I've listed you alphabetically because you're all equally important). A special thanks, also, to Diane Brown, Wendy Fick, Tonia Powell, Doug Pettinga, Julia Svoboda, Gary Barello, Chris Heaton, Mark Beardslee and Marci Giannosa. No one could ask for a better, more loyal staff.

For their friendship, support and inspiration, I thank my television coworkers, Carmen Harlan, Emery King, Chuck Gaidica, Ruth Spencer and Bernie Smilovitz.

Also, my production company colleagues, Ron Herman, Jeff Tottis and Gretchen Wnukowski.

Terry Oprea deserves *extra*-special thanks for his expert editing of the radio scripts and his superb directing of the radio feature, as does Suzanne Gougherty, without whose tireless efforts there would be no *Second Thoughts* radio network.

Ralph Mann of ICM, my close friend and longtime television agent, his wife, Bebe (Ralph, you're okay, but Bebe is prettier and smarter), and my terrific literary agent, Mitch Douglas. Ralph and Mitch, you're both great guys and true professionals.

Peter Vegso and Randee Goldsmith for their confidence in this book, and Marci Allen, who brought us together.

Lisa M. Bernstein for her careful and expert editing of the manuscript.

I'm also grateful to the following individuals for friendship, support and inspiration: Steve and Joyce Bell, Vince and Frankie Leonard, Robert and Alice Gustafson, Bob and Myrtle Everett, John Cruikshank III, Jeff Sangster, Rodger Young, Gene DeAgostino, Alan Frank, Bob Clinkingbeard, Paul Manzella, Jim Harper, Carol Rueppel, Tony Franco, Rick Inatome, Al Meltzer, Dr. John Burrows, Dr. Richard Mertz and the Reverend Bruce Rigdon.

Finally, for their faith in me and their support of *Second Thoughts,* Kmart's Floyd Hall, Warren Flick, Larry Davis and Shawn Kahle; and Chrysler's Bob Eaton and John MacDonald.

For those of you I've missed, you know who you are.

Please know how much I am indebted for your help.

(P.S. Pat Maday, thanks for never, *never* allowing *Second Thoughts* to be preempted! You're a man of incomparable judgment and taste.)

Introduction

I was on a news assignment in Central America.

My corner hotel room in Guatemala City had two windows.

One opened out over a beautiful green park.

The other, over an asphalt rooftop and below that, an alley.

I had a choice. I could look out at the park and enjoy the attractive landscape with its fascinating panorama of people having a good time.

Or I could stare down at the bleak scene of tar roof and trashy alley.

Every day offers us similar choices.

We can *select* whether to focus on the *good*—or on the *bad and the ugly.*

This collection of essays represents my choice.

They celebrate the good in the world.

They proclaim the potential of human beings to make a difference.

As a journalist for more than 30 years, I've seen my share of the bad and the ugly. It's real. And we need to address it.

But I've seen many other realities. Acts of personal heroism. Sacrifice. Love.

Four years ago I began a national radio series called *Second Thoughts*. It is a daily reflection on the best in the world and the power we possess to change what's not so good.

This book is published in direct response to the thousands of requests we've received for *Second Thoughts* scripts.

It is the author's firm conviction that, for all our problems, there's still a lot more good in the world than bad.

More reason for hope than for despair.

SECOND THOUGHTS

Security—And Opportunity

How do we make our children feel secure in a world that isn't?

Tarzan was right.

It *is* a jungle out there.

As parents, we'd like to defuse the dangers faced by our children.

We wish there were no diseases, accidents, crime or economic uncertainty to threaten their future.

Obviously, there's not much we can do about the *kind* of world they face. But there's a lot we can do about the *way* they face it.

We can remind them that life, essentially, is no more dangerous now than it's ever been.

The threat of nuclear annihilation is less likely now than when most of us were growing up.

Better food production, nutrition, medical care and hygiene today contribute to life spans nearly twice what our ancestors could anticipate.

AIDS *is* scary, but it is preventable, and no more frightening than plagues of earlier times. Cholera. Scarlet fever. Tuberculosis. Polio.

Perhaps most importantly we can help our children understand that *danger* means challenge; that *risk* means there's exciting work to be done.

Charles Ricker, a management services executive, says he's lived his life on the basis that there's no such thing as security—only opportunity.

We can teach our children to be *answer*-oriented and to focus on solutions instead of fretting over problems.

If we can't make the future what we'd like it to be for our children, let's make them what they *need* to be for the future.

The Show *Can* Go On

You can survive an incredible plunge if you know how to fall!

Her parachute had only partially opened, and the sky diver hit the ground, hard. But at the hospital doctors discovered her injuries were amazingly slight.

"It's because I've been trained how to fall," she told me during an interview.

Learning how to fall can mean the difference between life and death. We were watching the world-renowned acrobatic troupe Cirque du Soleil as they performed in Las Vegas. The audience was fascinated to the point of awe by highly skilled performers flying from one swinging trapeze to another, twisting in midair, then grabbing the wrists of a partner swooping at them from another direction.

Suddenly one of the acrobats missed. There were gasps from the crowd as she plunged toward the net 50 to 60 feet below. But with the grace and precision of a ballet dancer, the falling performer turned her body so that she landed on the net in full control. She hit the net in sort of a half-prone position.

Despite slamming into the net at considerable speed, she bounced back upright onto both feet, hopped over to the rope ladder and climbed back up to the trapeze. Her skill in taking that fall was every bit as impressive as her ability on the swings.

None of us gets through life without taking some falls.

We tumble off the career ladder.

We stumble in our marriages.

We get knocked flat by unexpected illness or accident.

We are tripped up by financial reverses.

We may be dazed. We may even be hurt.

But if we've learned how to fall, we *can* get up again.

Our show *can* go on!

Room for Improvement

**It's tough enough to admit
our faults to ourselves.
It's even tougher when *others*
discover we aren't perfect!**

Nick George was one of the toughest editors ever to darken the desk of a rookie writer.

When Nick slipped up behind you, pipe protruding from clenched teeth, a scowl on his rugged face, you could feel the cold, critical eye before you heard the first rumble.

Working in his newsroom was like living on a verbal fault line: You knew the earthquake was inevitable—you just didn't know when.

But once you got to know Nick, you understood that he *criticized* because he *cared*. He cared about words. About phrasing. About facts. About *truth.* Much of what I learned about clear, concise newswriting I learned because Nick George was a tough critic.

Criticism isn't easy to take. But there's no progress without it.

It's so easy for us to take criticism personally, to let our egos cloud our intelligence and distort our judgment.

I have a workshop in my garage for that occasional household repair. Once in a great while I even fancy myself a carpenter and try to build something. I've learned over the years that the *rougher* the board, the *coarser* the sandpaper I have to use. That's the only way to smooth it out.

Life works better at school, on the job or in the home when we learn to appreciate criticism and benefit from it.

If we truly want to grow, to develop and to improve, we not only should accept criticism, we should insist on it.

After all, the biggest room in the world is the room for improvement.

Advertising Works

Ever thought about producing your own commercials?

Whether we think so or not, all of us are influenced by advertising.

If advertising weren't a powerful persuader, corporations wouldn't spend billions of dollars every year to sell their products on radio, television, billboards, flyers, the Internet, the sides of buses, in newspapers and in scores of other media.

Advertising *works* because it puts suggestions into our minds.

You're at the store. You're looking at paper towels. You don't have any particular brand in mind. But as you think about it, a subtle voice in your head says, "Choose *that* brand."

Somewhere in your subconscious, you've just been *reached* by that company's advertising.

But why let *others* dictate all the ads that will influence us? Why not employ advertising ourselves? Create our own commercials for issues or projects or improvements important to us, then use them to plant ideas in our own subconscious?

First thing in the morning and last thing at night, you might suggest something *really positive* to yourself.

Maybe you'll want to do a little print advertising. Write it out on a card or a piece of paper:

Today I will watch my fat intake.

Today I will exercise for 15 minutes.

Today I will show up to work 10 minutes early.

And just as the major corporations do, repeat the ad to yourself several times a day.

Whatever you're trying to sell yourself, remember that advertising works.

Try it. You'll buy it.

A Horse Named Never Despair

**When you're at the end of your rope,
just tie a knot and hang on!**

S tubbornness can be irritating.

It can also be lifesaving.

I recall leading a newscast one evening with the story of a very stubborn man. His Jet Ski had stopped running, and he was too far from shore for anyone to see or hear him.

The sun baked his skin as currents carried him farther and farther out to sea.

Finally he could no longer see land, and for nearly three days and nights he drifted.

But he never gave up. He hung on, stubbornly, and eventually was spotted by the crew of a ship and rescued.

What if he'd given up just one hour before help arrived?

Fortunately it wasn't this man's nature to quit. And so he hung on.

How many entrepreneurs have succeeded simply because they hung in there a little longer after everyone was telling them it was no use? No matter how tough it was, they were too stubborn to let despair take over.

A woman in lower Manhattan was a soft touch for anyone down on his luck. One morning she took pity on the man she'd seen standing on a corner near her apartment. He looked so forlorn, and she wanted to encourage him.

Pressing a dollar into his hand, she whispered, "Never despair."

Next day as she passed him, the man stopped the woman and handed her *nine* dollars.

"What's this?" she asked.

"It's your winnings," the man responded.

Yes, you guessed it. The object of this woman's charity was a bookie, and a horse named Never Despair had won at 8-1.

In the great race of life it's an even better bet that Never Despair will always finish in the money.

The Trade-Off

We can't have it all.
But we *can* have enough.

The message comes from a variety of sources:
Seminars.
Self-help books and tapes.
Even some commencement addresses.

The message is: You can have it all. Be everything. Do everything. And you can be and do it all at the same time if only you follow the right formula.

It's a seductive message and one we would like to believe.

The problem is, it's not true. Despite its popular appeal, it's a message that doesn't work in the real world.

People who do realize their dreams and reach their goals are those who recognize that life demands trade-offs.

They've figured out that everything has a price.

There's a Chinese proverb that goes something like this: *Walk into the great store of life and take what you want. But be prepared to pay for it.*

It's human nature to *want* it all—and all at the same time.

We want maximum freedom, but we also crave law and order. The reality is that one comes at the expense of the other. The cost of *total* order is a loss of liberty. During the darkest days of Communist oppression Soviet citizens certainly had order. But they did not have freedom. When they traded off some of that *order* for increased *freedom,* many were unprepared for the exchange.

This trade-off principle works in our personal lives, too. Every decision opens one door and closes others:

When you decide to attend a particular college, take a specific job or marry a certain person, by that decision you have eliminated other possibilities.

Living is like editing a newspaper. Any editor knows that not every story can be printed. There's only so much news space, so even good stories sometimes have to be eliminated.

We live in a world of assets and liabilities.

Of promise and peril.

Of opportunity and opposition.

We *can have* what we want so long as we don't want everything at once.

We *can be* what we want so long as we understand the trade-offs and are willing to pay the price.

Lower the Backboard

Big dreams are terrific.
Impossible dreams are terrible.
It pays to know the difference.

When our son was five years old we moved into a home with a basketball hoop mounted on the garage.

A couple of times Al tried to put the ball through the hoop but never could get it more than halfway. His little arms simply weren't strong enough.

I decided what he needed was a basketball hoop low enough so that his shots would have a chance. So we dropped the backboard a couple of feet.

It worked. Al grabbed the basketball and fired it toward the rim. His first few tosses were short. But eventually he dropped one in and from that moment began to enjoy the game.

A neighbor, who'd helped me lower the backboard, said, "You know, even a child has to have attainable goals."

As Al grew, we moved the goal back up.

All of us respond better when the goals we set, or those set for us by others, are within reach.

Have you ever taken on a project that you simply didn't have the patience, the knack or the means to see through? Maybe you tackled it for the wrong reason: to please your husband or wife. Or because you thought it was "expected."

Pursuing *excellence* can be gratifying because excellence is attainable.

But aiming for *perfection* can only lead to disillusionment and despair because perfection is an impossible goal.

The very first test to which we should subject any personal goal is this: Do I have *any* chance of achieving it?

It's possible that we need to *lower the backboard* a bit.

Let our *dreams* grow as *we* grow.

As our young son learned from a basketball, what seems impossible today may well be within reach—tomorrow.

"I Can Deal with That"

**There's only one thing to
do when your world falls apart:
put it back together.**

Fairy tales are wonderful because they always have the
prince and the princess living happily ever after.

Of course life isn't a fairy tale. And in the real world the
prince may run off with his secretary; the princess may walk
out on the family to find herself; the royal offspring may do
drugs; and a downsizing at the plant may leave the entire family on the brink of bankruptcy.

So how do we keep from coming unglued when our whole
world is falling apart?

We start by facing the reality that life is not fair and then
respond, boldly, *So what! I can deal with that.*

Once we accept the fact that bad things do happen to good
people, then we can get on with the business of living life to
the fullest: giving, loving, creating, sharing, building, walking
through every door of opportunity offered by this fragile,
unpredictable, exciting experience called life.

If we live long enough, we'll all suffer personal losses. Financial setbacks. Disappointments in relationships. Illness. Accidents. Death.

But if we accept life with its wonderful possibilities—if we reach out to those who care about our pain—we can recover from our deepest hurts, bounce back from our hardest falls and experience healing of our most profound sorrows.

So, life *isn't* always fair.

So what!

7,000 Tennis Balls

**Did you know that
failing at something doesn't
mean *you* are a failure?**

B ruce Barrett was my tennis instructor. Bruce told me he had hit an estimated 7,000 tennis balls, trying to perfect one new serve.

How many of those serves were failures? That depends upon your viewpoint: To the extent that every *bad* serve helped him find the *good* one, none, ultimately, was a failure.

There was a young man who lost his job and the very same year was defeated when he ran for the state legislature.

A year later his business failed. He finally did win an election, but the following year the woman he loved died.

The year after that he had a nervous breakdown and suffered two more political defeats before finally winning a seat in Congress. But his bid for renomination was unsuccessful, and then he was defeated when he ran for the U.S. Senate.

This same man later tried to get himself nominated as vice president. He failed. He made another run for the Senate. He lost.

But here's the interesting part of the story: It is not for all those defeats, setbacks and failures that we remember this man. For eventually, despite all those failures, Abraham Lincoln scored a success.

Because he never stopped trying, Lincoln must have understood that experiencing a failure is not the same as being a failure.

Did your job not work out? That doesn't mean *you* are a failure.

Did your marriage fall apart? That doesn't mean *you* are a failure.

Deficiencies and defeats should be seen as stepping stones, not stumbling blocks.

Everybody feels the pain of failures.

Only the wise are able to learn from them.

And move on.

"I'm Good Because I Golf"

**What gave Lee Trevino
the winning edge in golf can give
you the winning edge in life!**

L ee Trevino had been winning one seniors' tournament after another.

Sure, we knew Lee was a great golfer. But so were the other veterans on the tour.

Why was Lee standing out? The talk-show host wanted to know.

"Simple answer," Lee said. "Golf is my life. After winning the other evening, I went back to the golf course the next morning to take 350 practice swings. Most everybody else went off to other places."

Then Lee Trevino shared a success secret understood by all champions. He said, "I'm good because I golf."

Superachievers in every field understand the necessity of doing what they do again and again, never becoming complacent or overconfident.

During a backstage interview, the late Benny Goodman told me he continued to practice the clarinet several hours every day to keep his lip in shape, to stay sharp. Benny Goodman was well into his 70s, still performing brilliant concerts, still working day after day, honing his skills.

Athletes, musicians, entrepreneurs—those who make it big —all share this drive toward continual improvement. For them just being good enough is never *good enough.*

Truly successful people are always reaching and stretching. In the immodest but immortal words of Lee Trevino, "I'm good because I golf."

Seizing the Moment

The best answer to missed opportunity is to catch it the next time around.

Advertisements and popular opinion aside, there really are very few "once-in-a-lifetime" opportunities.

Most opportunities come knocking several times, although we may have to be alert because they don't always knock loudly.

If we could truly believe this, then we'd waste far less energy on life's *if onlys*.

We all know the litany:

If only I'd completed college.

If only I'd taken that job 10 years ago.

If only I'd started my own business.

Bought that land.

Married that special person.

The *if only* list can seem endless. For the most part it's a foolish waste of time and not worth all the regret it generates.

The important question is not "What opportunities did I miss yesterday?" but rather "What doors are opening in front of me right now?"

Ray Kroc was 52 years old when he began the business we know today as McDonald's.

My good friend, the late Harland Sanders, was 65 when he launched Kentucky Fried Chicken.

How many times do you think opportunity knocked before these men finally answered the door?

How many once-in-a-lifetime chances do you think they blew before seizing the moment?

For part of his life my father was a college counselor. One day a woman who was down on herself for not having completed college came to see him. Dad urged her to go back, but she was frustrated by her age, believing she was too old.

"Dr. Crim," she said, "I'm 55. It would take five years to get my degree, and in five years I'll be 60."

Dad smiled and replied, "Well, if you don't get your degree, how old will you be in five years?"

Hockey star Wayne Gretzky notes: "You miss 100 percent of the shots you never take."

Of course a good player like Gretzky doesn't concentrate on missed shots.

It's the ones still to be *taken* that count.

A Strategy, a Design, a Map

**If you don't know where
you're going, you may end up
where you're headed.**

When she was four, our daughter was working at her blackboard. I looked at the scrawl marks and asked, "Carey, what are you drawing?"

Without stopping, she looked at her picture and said, "I don't know, Dad. I'll figure out what it is after I've finished it."

Is it possible that, as adults, we live out the days of our lives like that? Making our marks but not really sure what they mean without a master plan or a vision to guide us?

Interesting, isn't it, that many of us spend more time planning a two-week vacation than we do planning our lives?

You have to do more than work hard at life to succeed. You have to work smart. That means first and foremost: You need a plan.

No sensible contractor would begin building a house without a blueprint. Pilots and sailors rely upon charts.

Entrepreneurs create business plans. All of us need a strategy, a design, a map if we're to realize our potential in life.

Successful careers, successful marriages, successful child-rearing do not come about by accident or luck.

The secret to reaching any goal is first to define the goal, then work out a logical, practical plan for attaining it.

Michael Jordan, in explaining why he'd majored in geography at the University of North Carolina, said it was because "I knew that I would be going places, and I just wanted to know where I was when I got there."

When God Closes a Door . . .

**Unexpected detours in life can
lead to the best roads of all!**

When our teenage daughter broke up with her first
boyfriend, she was crushed. And sensing *her* pain
made it almost worse for her parents.

But we did have the benefit of the knowledge that comes
with experience. We knew that a first love rarely is the last
and that later our daughter would likely look back on that
juvenile heartbreak and smile.

Early in my career there was a job that I desperately
wanted. When it didn't work out, I was devastated. Now I
recognize that getting that position would have thwarted my
career. The detour I was forced to take led to great opportunities that I couldn't have foreseen.

I don't know who first said it, but life experience seems to
validate it: *When God closes a door, he opens a window.*

Has the door just been slammed on your career? Your
marriage? Your health? Your hopes for the future?

If it seems you're at a dead end, look closely. It may be only an intersection. This may be the time to see if there aren't some other roads leading off in different directions.

People who succeed in love or in life don't get hung up on which route will get them to their destination.

In geometry a straight line is the shortest distance between two points. But life isn't a mathematical equation.

We can't always zip along on life's expressways. Sometimes we're forced onto side roads. When that happens, it's always wise to keep a steady hand on the wheel and a keen eye open for important signs along the way.

Eventually we'll reach our destination.

Who knows, this might prove to be a more scenic, more interesting route!

Sweating the Small Stuff

Why do we feel so bad when we've got it so good?

A doctor was telling me this week about a speech he delivers to fellow physicians. He titles his talk "Why Do We Feel So Bad When We've Got It So Good?"

He chides his colleagues for grousing about prospective changes in the medical care system. No matter what Congress does or doesn't do, he argues, we'll still have the best medical care in the world—and the highest-paid doctors. So what are his physician friends so worried about?

He believes it's the same thing that has all of us worried: *change.* Any change is unsettling. We get comfortable with the way things are, even if we know they could be improved.

Maybe that's why all of us at times feel bad despite the fact that we've got it good. Right now we're caught up in a whirlpool of the most sweeping changes in history.

Life not only is changing dramatically, the changes are occurring at warp speed—at home, at school and in the workplace.

Sometimes we feel as though a truck's barreling down on us along the information superhighway while we're pulled off on the side of the road trying to figure out how to program our VCRs.

So it's small wonder our emotions often seem out of sync with the reality of our situation; that we may feel uneasy or sad despite having a pretty good job, a nice family and reasonably good health.

I suspect my doctor friend is correct about the reason for this paradox: It's simply that so much is happening to us and around us so fast. *Too* fast.

Maybe it's time to invoke those famous two rules for beating anxiety:

Rule number one: Don't sweat the small stuff.

Rule number two: It's all small stuff.

Yu Bee's Mountain

**The mountains *some* people
have to climb make *ours*
look like molehills!**

The restaurant was only a few weeks old, but business was
already brisk.

"This place seems to be doing very well," I commented to
the waitress as she brought our check.

"Oh, he'll make it," she said as she motioned toward a
small Asian man working the cash register. "He and his family climbed a mountain to get here."

I presumed this was her way of saying that the people
who'd built this restaurant had faced lots of obstacles: finding
a suitable location, obtaining financing and so on.

"Yes, starting any business is quite a hill to get over," I
responded.

"I'm talking about a *real* mountain," she explained. "This
man, his wife and two children literally had to crawl up the
side of a mountain before they could escape from Cambodia."

The waitress then told us that Yu Bee and his family were boat people. They had risked their lives to flee Cambodia when it was still under Communist control.

"You can't believe their work ethic," our waitress went on. "These folks will stay here until one or two in the morning. Every night they scrub down every inch of the kitchen.

"And they're so grateful. I've never known people so enthusiastic about America and the opportunities they've found here."

It makes you wonder whether you and I would be less cynical about our nation and have fewer complaints about our way of life if we could see America through the eyes of those who've experienced the alternatives.

People like Yu Bee and his family.

People who climbed a mountain to get here.

"The Natives Don't Wear Shoes"

**Our greatest underdeveloped
natural resource is *us*.**

M any years ago, as a cub reporter, I covered an amazing story.

At first it appeared to be a routine traffic accident. An overturned car. But there was a woman trapped underneath.

Two young men traveling right behind had jumped from their car, grabbed hold of the overturned vehicle and, with superhuman strength, lifted more than a ton of steel to free the woman.

These weren't weight lifters or wrestlers. They weren't athletes of any kind—just a couple of ordinary men who recognized a crisis and did what had to be done. Later, when I interviewed them, both said they had been surprised by their own strength. They never would have dreamed themselves capable of doing what they did.

Most of us are shackled by limiting notions of our own effectiveness. We may be convinced we lack talent. Or brainpower. Or we don't have enough time. Or family and friends won't cooperate with our aspirations.

So we continue to live our ordinary lives in ordinary ways, afraid to challenge the limitations set for us by ourselves or others.

Every day, for each of us, there are opportunities to make life better. But we have to be *tuned in* to possibilities.

A few years ago an American shoe company sent two salesmen to the Australian outback. They wanted to find out whether there was any market for shoes among the Aborigines.

They received telegrams from both salesmen.

The first said, "No business here. The natives don't wear shoes."

But the second telegram proclaimed, "Great opportunity here. The natives don't wear shoes."

The second salesman understood that a problem may be nothing more than an opportunity in disguise.

A Fresh Perspective

**To get a good look at our own lives,
we may need to see our reflections
in the images others have of us.**

"**N**ew tie?" one of my colleagues asked.

"No, actually I've had it for several years. But I haven't worn it in a while."

Several times that day people complimented that necktie.

The irony is that I'd almost gotten rid of it. I had owned that tie for so long that to me it was starting to look old. It had lost its flair. But this, apparently, was not the way others saw it.

How often is our own perception of reality limited by our closeness to a situation? By our familiarity with it?

The friends of a young man I know were baffled by his decision to leave his wife. From all we could determine, she was a lovely woman, physically attractive, kind and with a terrific personality. That's how others perceived her. But he was so close to the situation, he evidently couldn't see the outstanding qualities that seemed so clear to his friends.

That's why it's sometimes helpful to seek the opinions of those we trust. And listen to them. Often they can give us a fresh perspective. A more objective analysis. They just may help us see the value of something we've started taking for granted. It may be something as trivial as a necktie. It may be as significant as a marriage or a job that has started to bore us.

An acquaintance of mine owned a home in a fashionable suburb of New York. He decided to sell it and had his broker place an ad in the *New York Times*. But the next Sunday, after reading the ad, he called his broker and said, "Take my house off the market. After reading that ad, I've decided this is exactly the kind of house I've been looking for all my life."

Moving on Up

**It was the theme song
for a popular television series.
It's also the American way of life.**

"**M**oving on Up" was the theme song for TV's *The Jeffersons*. But the concept is older than George Jefferson. Even older than Thomas Jefferson.

Moving up has been a dominant theme in American life since the nation's founding.

Unlike the former Soviet Union, the United States has never sought to be a classless society.

The founders of this unique experiment in democracy never believed they could eliminate the various social and economic levels. What they *did* set out to do was open up the system. Provide doors of opportunity so that no one had to be stuck at the bottom.

From then until now a major hallmark of America has been its upward mobility.

We needn't search history books or dig for Horatio Alger

stories to find compelling accounts of Americans who pulled themselves up from rags to riches.

Many were immigrants who left their homelands precisely because those countries provided little or no such upward mobility.

And here's some encouraging news: The list of people climbing the ladder of success today includes a growing number of women and members of ethnic minorities.

One of the keys to upward mobility in America is our unique system of investment and financing. Anyone with a new idea can seek a backer and become an entrepreneur. Sometimes the results are amazing.

Sometimes, humorous:

His colleagues held a dinner honoring a European immigrant who'd built an enormous business in his city. When it came time for him to speak, the old gentleman stood at the microphone and said:

"Folks, I guess I'm a typical American success story. Fifty years ago I landed in this great country without a dime.

"Tonight, I stand before you—$50 million in debt."

"Practice, Son, Practice"

**The cost of anything is rarely
just the price we pay.**

When I was 16, I bought an airplane.

I'd worked two summers in construction to save the $475 that the plane cost. By today's standards it wasn't much of an airplane. About as basic as you could imagine. No electrical system. You got it started by hand-cranking the propeller.

But that yellow, fabric-covered, two-seat Aeronca was a dream come true for me. It was mine. I had bought it and paid for it. I could hardly wait to take it off the ground.

Of course the *real* price of flying wasn't what I'd paid for the plane. The freedom to fly carried a different price tag: extensive and tedious study, ground school, dual instruction and hours of practicing takeoffs and landings. When you totaled these, they were what it cost me to fly. Buying that plane was only a down payment.

There's an old joke about a boy who asks a street vendor in New York how to get to Carnegie Hall. The vendor replies, "Practice, son, practice."

But the joke contains a serious message.

So much of what we want from life is attainable *for a price.*

To achieve our most important goals, inevitably the price includes work. Discipline. Persistence. The cost of true success is always more than money can buy.

We may envy the colleague who has the freedom to vacation in the Caribbean or buy a new car every couple of years. But what personal price has that person paid for such success? What looks like good fortune more than likely is a combination of study, training, dedication and long hours.

In life as in business we tend to get what we pay for.

And it's always a good idea to be prepared for some hidden costs.

The Common Sense of the Common Man

The *extraordinary* thing
about America is how much faith
we place in *ordinary* people.

For all of our frustration with Congress, our system of representative government remains the best so far devised.

Winston Churchill certainly would have understood our impatience with corruption, self-dealing, smelly political contributions, legislative incompetence and gridlock.

He was expressing the ambivalence all of us feel at times when he proclaimed democracy the worst form of government except for all the others that have been tried.

Believing in the common sense of the common man or woman is a bold and *un*common concept. It is not without risk or frustration.

But the alternative to letting citizens decide their own future is, of course, to allow a single dictator or an elite corps of experts to decide. And history proves that kings, czars and commissars are poor substitutes for rule by the people.

We see a demonstration of our system's uniqueness every time Congress meets. For such a weighty matter as making our nation's laws, we wisely bring in these amateurs. Not experts, but simply representatives of the people—like us—chosen from all walks of life.

When we want something *less* important done, like sending astronauts to the moon, we call in the specialists, the experts.

Or look at our criminal justice system. How interesting that we consider a man's guilt or innocence of such supreme importance that we won't leave *that* to the experts, either.

So we pick average citizens like you and me to sit on a jury. Not people trained in the law. Not judicial authorities. Just common citizens who can listen and feel and react to what they see and hear.

There in our courtrooms, where the most serious matters of life and death may be decided, we give the job to 12 ordinary people.

Come to think of it, isn't that what the founder of Christianity did?

Living Within the Lines

If your life were art, would it be a canvas? Or a coloring book?

I once read that some psychologists claim they can tell quite a lot about children's personalities from the way they color in a coloring book.

Some will apply their crayons meticulously inside the lines.

Less inhibited youngsters will color outside the lines, and a few free spirits will create their own lines.

Successful living requires both. To be sure, there are rules that must be observed if we're to get along in life:

Showing up on time for work.

Stopping at red lights.

Paying our bills.

Waiting our turn.

These are all lines society has drawn, and without *some* lines there could be no order and ultimately no civilization.

But life can get pretty dull if we never do anything outside the lines.

If life is part coloring book, it's also part canvas, offering us an opportunity to sketch our own views of reality, apply our own colors and our own textures.

I discovered an oil painting in the attic that one of our children had made in grade school. It was one of those paint-by-the-numbers pictures.

You may remember when they were popular. You began with a canvas that had a picture already sketched. There were tiny boxes and a number assigned for each brush stroke. The lines showed you where to paint, and the numbers dictated each color. The final result was okay, but it always had a mechanical look to it. With both lines and colors predetermined by someone else, there was no room for spontaneity. No originality.

Some of life has to be lived within the lines.

But like painting by the numbers, if we never venture outside the lines—never choose our own colors—then life can be incredibly boring, uninspiring and ultimately unfulfilling.

No Fear of Flying

**It almost killed him.
So he did it again.
Sometimes that's the best way.**

Bob Hoover may be the greatest aerobatics pilot alive.

He's been a test pilot, combat pilot and prisoner of war.

He's wrestled out-of-control jet fighters back to the ground, fought fires in the air and crashed more times than he can count.

One crash during a test flight of a Super Sabre jet broke Hoover's back and almost killed him. Just as soon as he recovered, Bob Hoover climbed into the cockpit of another Super Sabre and took it up for another test flight. As he tells it in his easy Tennessee drawl, "You gotta get back into the cockpit of the bird that bit ya."

While Hoover is courageous and willing to take risks, he's not foolhardy or reckless. If he were, he wouldn't be alive today. But Hoover knows that any fear we don't defeat will defeat us.

So he determined to face down his fear.

Wally Amos, who became a multimillionaire with his Famous Amos chocolate chip cookies, puts it another way: He believes there have been no negative experiences in his life because in his view there's a lesson within every experience.

Whether you crash in a plane, get thrown from a horse, go bankrupt, or find your marriage or career falling apart, you have the same choice to make:

Allow fear to paralyze you.

Or, as Bob Hoover would say, "Get back into the cockpit of the bird that bit ya."

Wishers and Winners

**Only one small word separates
those who get things done from
those who don't: *do!***

If you don't believe success is mostly a matter of luck, just ask anyone who's failed. They'll tell you, "Hey, with a few good breaks, I could have achieved something."

Achievement is not the result of lucky breaks. The crucial difference between those who accomplish and those who don't is rarely a roll of the dice. It's simply that achievers *do it* while others *dream* about it.

It's so easy to *say* what we're going to do. To dream of doing. Fantasize. Plan. Talk. Get *ready* to do.

But actually doing it—that's what separates *winners* from *wishers.*

How many people have a book inside their head just waiting to be written?

Libraries couldn't contain all the novels if suddenly every aspiring author actually wrote one.

As someone who does write for a living, I have this caution taped to my desk.

It says: "Planning to write is not writing. Thinking about writing is not writing. Talking about writing is not writing. Researching to write, outlining to write—none of this is writing. *Writing* is writing."

When asked if he only wrote when inspired, a famous author told our journalism class, "Yes, I write only when inspired. And I make certain that I'm inspired every morning from 8:00 until 11:00."

This principle applies to everything: Doing is doing. There is no substitute. No other way to achieve.

The world is ready and waiting for people who'll put their dreams to work.

And *those* people will find the competition not nearly as tough as they'd imagined.

Because so many potential competitors will do everything it takes to succeed.

Except to *do it!*

Back It with Action

**Wishes *can* work.
But only if *we* do!**

A nn Wise had spent many years as a secretary, but always her goal was to own her own business.

Then one morning there it was in the newspaper: a feature story detailing how this hardworking, ambitious young woman had realized her dream.

Ann wanted to establish an auto repair service employing only women mechanics. For years she'd felt either ignored or insulted by male mechanics who wouldn't or couldn't explain the work they were doing. And when they did, they always seemed to be talking down to her. Their attitude seemed to say, "What could a woman possibly know about a car?"

Now Ann was realizing her dream because she'd backed it with action.

When I went by her office to congratulate her, she explained how much work had been involved—developing a business plan, finding backers and locating the skilled women mechanics.

But she'd done it, and her customers—mostly female—loved it.

Whether our wish is to improve a relationship, advance on the job, start a business or develop some new skill, the formula is the same: hook up the emotional jumper cables and jolt ourselves into action.

The secretary-turned-entrepreneur understood that. A budding author in New York apparently did not. When his landlady reminded him that his rent was a month overdue, he said, "I'll pay you just as soon as I get the check that the publisher's sending me if he accepts the novel I'm about to write once I've found a good subject and get the necessary inspiration."

Wishes do work.

But only if *we work* at them.

A Most Valuable Resource

There ought to be a law against killing time.

T ime is the great equalizer.

Everybody starts the day with the same 24 hours staring them in the face.

It doesn't matter how rich you are or how poor. Whether you work in an office or a factory or don't work at all. Time plays no favorites with people or positions.

Success in life depends heavily upon how well we learn to use this most valuable, nonrenewable resource. Once it's gone, whether invested wisely or squandered foolishly, it can never be recaptured.

That's why, in my view, killing time should be a capital offense. Just think what can be—and is—accomplished by people who've learned to utilize that odd moment, to collect and exploit an extra hour here and there. People have earned college degrees and pilot's licenses, written books and started businesses simply by taking advantage of spare time.

It wasn't that they had any more time than the next person. They may not necessarily have been brighter or more talented. They simply recognized what can be done when time is respected and invested.

What is it in your life that you *think* you don't have time for?

Would you like to learn computers? Become a beautician? A photographer? Improve your parenting skills? Become an accountant? I've seen the power of pulling together wasted minutes and hours. There's plenty of evidence that we can do just about anything we want to do in our spare time.

That is, once we stop *killing* it.

"Lots of Time to Prepare"

**Sometimes the winner is
simply the person who *sticks with it*
a little longer!**

People younger than baby boomers may have difficulty remembering when Lawrence Welk had one of the most popular shows on television.

Welk hit stardom back when most TV pictures were black and white, the dialogue was never blue and everything was live.

He was well into his 60s by the time his show took off, although he'd been a bandleader for decades.

Lawrence Welk once told a reporter he thought he'd lasted so long precisely because success came to him late. That, he said, had given him lots of time to prepare.

Longevity isn't everything, of course, but without perseverance, neither talent nor genius will take a person very far. Many people of average ability or intelligence have achieved extraordinary success by sticking with it longer than their competition.

I read this week that the average entrepreneur who makes it big has previously failed four times.

Theodor Geisel's first book was turned down by 28 publishers before Vanguard finally accepted it.

After that Geisel went on to write 46 other books, including two that you're sure to recognize: *The Cat in the Hat* and *Green Eggs and Ham.*

We know Theodor Geisel, of course, by his pen name: Dr. Seuss.

Perhaps Geisel's greatest story wasn't one he wrote. It was the one he lived—the story of determination and perseverance.

The story of a writer who simply stuck with it a little longer.

Stir It Up

If you're living a life of quiet desperation, stop that! Make some noise. Reignite the spark!

One of modern life's strangest ironies is boredom.

Never have humans been so inundated with diversions.

Sports and hobby shops offer us enough equipment to keep our bodies and our minds fit for a lifetime.

Department store shelves bulge with grown-up toys from bread makers to camcorders.

We can indulge in any hobby from stamp collecting to scuba diving. From model railroading to fishing. From antiques to computers. There are books and videos and clubs to support every interest we ever imagined and some we couldn't.

But here's the irony: Despite all our sports, avocations and hobbies, many of us remain incredibly bored.

We have access to variety, but we practice *routine.*

When life grows stale, it's because we've allowed it to.

The only way to keep life from becoming dull is to stir it up once in a while.

Do we drive the same exact route to work every day? We should check out a different route some morning.

Do we read the same magazines month after month? Why not buy something we haven't read before? Perhaps a magazine about a subject we know little about.

Do we always watch the same TV shows? Read the same kinds of books? Talk about the same subjects? Then it's time to try something different. Even wearing different kinds of clothing can change our *outlook* as well as our look.

Don't become too predictable. Don't let your spirit die before you do.

The only difference between a rut and a grave is the length.

At Least Buy a Ticket

There are two kinds of people in the world: those who call the shots and those who dodge the bullets.

The world *is* a stage, but not all people are actors. Some are *re*actors. They only *react* to conditions instead of creating them.

Such people wait passively for life to happen. Then they wonder why, so often, the wrong things happen.

On the other hand, people who act, who take charge of their lives, who decide what they want and then go after it—these people find that *good* things happen.

In relationships or in work, we can't always wait for our ship to come in. Sometimes we have to swim out to meet it.

It's a well-established principle in business that successful executives are the ones who act rather than react, who stay ahead of the game, playing *offense* rather than *defense.*

It's amazing how, when you begin to act decisively, obstacles start to fall and luck begins to favor you.

Still, many of us are slow to get the message.

For instance, the man who became so desperate after his business failed that he decided to try prayer. He'd never been particularly religious, but how could it hurt?

So he prayed, "Dear God, you've got to help me. The only way I can get back on my feet is to win the lottery."

Day after day he'd pray this same prayer, "Please, God, all I need is to win the lottery."

Finally after one of these earnest petitions he heard a voice say:

"Give me a break. At least buy a ticket."

The Great Juggling Act

Do you manage your schedule, or does it manage you?

If Moses came down from the mountain today, this is how we anchormen would report it on television:

"Good evening. The Lord God Almighty has just issued 10 commandments. Here are three of the most important."

All of us spend a significant amount of time juggling and prioritizing as we try to figure out what's the *most* important.

Some of us need lists just to keep track of our lists.

One morning when our son was in grade school, I had brought my briefcase full of papers to the breakfast table. Al looked at his mom and said, "If Dad can't keep up at work, why don't they do him like they do us in school and put him in a slower group?"

Has any of us really found that *slower group?*

Easing the pace of our lives seems to be an almost universal desire. If only we had more time. An extra couple of hours a day to read, meditate or exercise. Time for ourselves. Our friends. Our hobbies. We're confident that if only we had additional time, we most certainly would use it wisely.

But would we?

What makes us think we'd invest *bonus* hours any differently than we do our current allotment?

When we're dead-on honest, don't we have to admit that we do with our *present* 24 hours essentially what we *want* to do?

We may say we're doing it for the boss or our spouse. We may *con* ourselves into believing the grueling pace of our lives is really for the children or for our friends or even for *the community.*

That's our defense. The truth is, how we invest our time is a matter of choice. And it's *our* choice.

We've studied the trade-offs. We've made the deals.

If we're juggling too many things, we truly can toss some of those things aside.

We can take charge of our own life.

We can make our own decisions.

We can learn to say *no* to things we don't want to do.

Or *yes* to things we want to do.

No excuses.

No blaming anyone else.

No grumbling about our circumstances.

Just a straight-up acceptance of personal responsibility for how we spend our time.

Respecting ourselves enough to take back our own daily calendars. It's a powerful first step for effective time management.

The Art of Nit-Picking

> **Any woman can tell you:**
> **Even Mr. *Right* will have a few**
> **things *wrong* with him.**

My dad was the classic optimist.

I think if he'd ever fallen into a lake, he would have come up checking his pockets for fish.

Some would contend that people like my father are just natural-*born* optimists. But I'm not so sure that a positive outlook comes from genes as much as it does from determination. Dad *worked* at seeing the best in people and situations. And that wasn't always easy.

What *is* easy is finding character defects in any personality. Human beings are complex. Most are neither all good nor all bad. And when we concentrate our attention on someone's failings, we can become blinded to much that is good and decent.

I recently read a biography about a scientist who was something of a cheat. It's now been documented that this man faked some of his data, stole a few ideas from other researchers and on top of that had a rather unpleasant personality. Most people—including his colleagues—didn't like him much.

But should all those flaws diminish our appreciation for what this man, Louis Pasteur, contributed to medicine? He is still the greatest scientist in French history.

In recent years it's become fashionable to focus on the flaws of our leaders. The news media have turned this negative nit-picking into a fine art!

It can also happen in personal relationships. And magnified or exaggerated faults can eclipse a lot of important *virtues.*

A real estate agent back East had the right idea.

"This property has advantages and disadvantages," he said.

"To the north is a gasworks, to the east a glue factory, to the south a fishery and to the west a sewage treatment plant."

"So," asked the customer, "what are the advantages?"

"Well," the agent answered, "you can always tell which way the wind's blowing."

How Much for That Piece of Lettuce?

**A thing doesn't have to
be big to be significant. Ever get
a speck of dirt in your eye?**

Several years ago a Lockheed L-1011 crashed into the Florida Everglades. The reason: a tiny gear indicator light. A small bulb that cost only a few cents. The crew got so busy with that small, burned-out bulb they forgot to fly the airplane.

Little things can have big consequences. They can also cost big money.

Delta Airlines once announced that it could save nearly $1.5 million dollars in food costs simply by eliminating the decorative piece of lettuce served under the vegetables on their in-flight meals.

It's easy to ignore little things, but sometimes it's those little things that are decisive. How many divorce judges or marriage counselors have heard the refrain "It seemed so insignificant at the time"?

We could overcome some of our biggest obstacles in life, enjoy some of our greatest successes and eliminate some of our worst fears if we'd pay more attention to little things.

A husband explained how he and his wife had agreed early in their marriage that he would make all the big decisions and she would make the less important ones.

When a friend asked how this worked he said: "Oh, I decide all the really *big* things, such as should we improve relations with China or should we change the health care system.

"My wife makes all the less important decisions, such as where we live, where we vacation and what kind of car we drive."

How often it is the so-called little things that make the biggest difference in our lives.

Action and Reaction

**Necessity is the mother of invention.
And a lot more!**

Bruce Barton, creative writer and advertising legend, delivered a lecture to an evening class in writing. Afterward one of his students asked, "Mr. Barton, where do you get the inspiration for your magazine articles?"

"Well," he replied, "picture me sitting at breakfast in the morning. As I sip my coffee, my wife across the table glances down at the floor and observes, 'Bruce, we really need a new dining room rug. This one is wearing through.' Right there I have the inspiration to write another article."

It probably wasn't what the students expected. No doubt they were disappointed with such an ordinary answer, little realizing that Bruce Barton had just shared with them one of the great secrets of motivation in virtually every field: *necessity.*

As a teenager I didn't need some outside source of motivation to *inspire* me to work. If I didn't get a job, I couldn't buy a bicycle. I couldn't take flying lessons. It was that simple. Necessity was the mother of my motivation.

Inspiration rarely strikes like a flash of lightning.

More often it's a conscious realization that what we *have* and what we *become* are direct consequences of what we *do*.

Motivation is understanding that behavior determines outcome.

We may want a better figure, more satisfying job, newer car, nicer house, better relationship with our spouse or children—but the motivation to achieve these goals isn't something that will miraculously happen. Motivation inevitably comes from within. It occurs when we finally make the connection between action and reaction.

Until we motivate ourselves, nobody can start us toward realization of our dreams.

When we do, nobody can stop us.

You Don't Need a Ph.D. to Be Happy

Since it's so *un*common these days, maybe we shouldn't call it *common* sense!

You know the type: a guy who's never made the same mistake twice but who's probably made all of them at least once.

The kind whose personnel file might contain this notation: *He is keenly analytical and his highly developed mentality could best be utilized in research and development. Footnote: He lacks common sense.*

Computers and calculators perform incredible functions, but they can never replace old-fashioned common sense.

And that's something you don't necessarily learn in school.

That's why we often meet college graduates who seem to be educated beyond their understanding.

You don't need a Ph.D. to live successfully and find happiness. But you do need the common sense that has brought meaning throughout the centuries to simple and sophisticated folk alike.

It's common sense that tells us:

Live every day to the fullest.

Be kind to your neighbor.

Be loyal to your family.

Be generous.

Base your life on trust, not anger or revenge.

Be positive.

Commit to your highest dreams. Don't succumb to your worst fears.

Take care of small things. Work hard. Strive for excellence.

These are principles our grandparents understood, as did their parents before them. Many were rural and poor. Simple and unsophisticated. Most had limited education. But their generations certainly weren't lacking in common sense.

Many college graduates today are startled when they get into the real world to discover how much supposedly uneducated people actually know.

And is there anybody quite as irritating as the person who has less training and fewer credentials than we have but abundantly more common sense?

"You Can Keep Your Blasted Lug Wrench!"

**Be careful what you wish for.
You may get it.**

There's incredible power in anticipation.

Not only do our expectations affect others, they strongly influence our own behavior.

My uncle Alvah was a great storyteller. One of his favorites was about a salesman driving along one dark, rainy night on a lonely country road when a tire went flat.

He opened the trunk. He had a spare tire but no lug wrench.

Noticing a light on in a farmhouse about a mile up the road, he decided to see whether he could borrow a wrench.

As the salesman sloshed his miserable way along the road, he got to thinking. His thoughts went something like this: "It's late at night. The farmer's asleep in a warm, dry bed. He may not even answer the door.

"Even if he does come to the door, he'll be angry that someone woke him up."

The salesman pressed on, his clothes now soaked, his socks

drenched. "If the farmer does come to the door, he'll probably shout, 'What's the big idea, waking me up at this hour?'"

That thought made the salesman *really* angry. What right did the farmer have to refuse a guy stranded in the middle of nowhere! The farmer was a selfish clod.

The salesman finally reached the house, banged on the door, and a light went on. A window popped open, and a voice said, "Who is it?"

By now the salesman was so worked up he yelled, "You know darn well who it is. It's me, and you can keep your blasted lug wrench! I wouldn't borrow it now if you had the last one on earth."

How often life deals us exactly the hand we expect.

"I Will Do It"

If you really want to do something, start by saying it!

Affirmations do affect actions.

When I handed our teenage son the car keys and said, "Now do be home by 12:00," he responded, "Well, Dad, I'll try."

His choice of words was a dead giveaway that he had little chance of meeting the midnight deadline.

"Son, what I'd like to hear you say is that you *will* be home by midnight."

The words we use in responding to a request or a challenge provide more than mere clues to our intent. The words actually affect the outcome. They may even predict it.

Weak words contribute to poor results. Strong words help bolster success. For instance, if you say, "Give me a call sometime," and I respond, "Okay, I'll try to do that," the chances are really high that you won't hear from me. *Try* is a weak word, and it inherently provides us with an *out*.

But if I say, "Okay, I will call you tomorrow before noon," then it's a good bet you'll hear from me in the morning.

Whenever we face a tough or distasteful job, our first challenge is convincing ourselves that we're up to it.

To declare with confidence "I will do it" provides us the momentum for ultimate success.

How many weekends my car has remained dirty, my garage a mess, because I told myself, "I'll try to get to them."

If you want to improve your batting average in life and enjoy a higher rate of success in everything you do, then make it a habit to say "I *will*."

If at first you don't succeed, don't *try* again.

Remember, there's no such word as *try*power. The word is *will*power.

The Real Competition

**In your race to succeed,
who do you think is your most
important rival?**

W e've been taught from infancy that competition is the
name of the game.

In school we compete for grades, for parts in plays, for
positions in the band or for a place on the team.

As we grow up, we compete for dates, for the college of our
choice and for a job.

By adulthood, rivalry has become such a way of life that we
find ourselves competing with our neighbors, our friends and
maybe even our spouses. It may start to bother us to see anyone wear better clothes, drive a nicer car, live in a bigger
house or earn more money than we do.

Some competition is healthy. Even necessary. But taken to
extremes it can sour friendships, ruin marriages, destroy
careers and devastate self-esteem.

I have a friend who doesn't *play* tennis. He *attacks* the
game.

And I once knew a golfer whose totally radical philosophy almost got him kicked out of a country club. He had this crazy notion that golf is *only a game.* Imagine!

A young first-year salesman I know mentioned during a telephone conversation with his mother that his company was giving the best accounts to older colleagues. He was having difficulty reaching their sales levels because they started out with this built-in advantage.

The young man's mother offered this wise advice:

"Don't worry about other salesmen. Don't compete with them. Forget what others *are* or *are not* doing. Compete with yourself. Try to sell more today than *you* sold yesterday."

What this mom had told her son came down to three essential words, and they contain the essence of a great success secret:

Compete with yourself.

Ultimately *that's* the competition that counts most.

"A Plowing Up of His Nature"

**Sometimes the *best* things
come from the *worst*
things that happen to us.**

There's not much need to go out deliberately looking for trouble. Usually it will find us without our help.

When it does, we try to dodge it, run from it or deny it.

But trouble *can* introduce us to hidden resources we didn't know we had.

In her biography of Franklin D. Roosevelt, Doris Kearns Goodwin tells how the paralysis that crippled FDR's body expanded his mind and his sensibilities.

After he contracted polio, he seemed less arrogant, less superficial and more interesting.

A friend of Roosevelt's observed there'd been *"a plowing up of his nature"*—that the man emerged with new humility of spirit and a firmer understanding.

Roosevelt certainly didn't go looking for the trouble polio brought to his life. But Goodwin believes that in some profound ways he benefited from it.

We usually can find something positive in every negative situation if we look for it. That certainly was true of a character described in one of Somerset Maugham's stories.

The man had been hired as a janitor at St. Peter's Church in London. One day a young vicar discovered that the janitor was illiterate and fired him.

Unable to find work elsewhere, the man took his meager savings and invested them in a tobacco shop. The shop did so well that eventually he bought another and kept expanding until he had a chain of tobacco stores worth several hundred thousand pounds—a fortune at that time.

One day the man's banker said, "You've done well for an illiterate. Just think where you'd be if you could read and write!"

The man thought for a moment. Then he said, "Well, I know where I'd be. I'd still be a janitor at St. Peter's Church."

Running on Empty?

Life isn't a problem to be solved.
It's an adventure to be enjoyed.

Here's a strange statistic: 18 percent of the private pilots who crash go down because of fuel exhaustion. In plain English, they run out of gas.

Strange, because running out of gas in an airplane seems so stupid. Yet last year 45 airplanes had unplanned encounters with the earth because of fuel exhaustion.

Certainly *these* accidents should be totally preventable. What kind of poor planning permits a pilot to run the plane's tanks dry?

Having flown for several decades, I ask this question rhetorically whenever I read that one of my fellow fliers has hit the ground with the gauges on empty.

But before we become too critical of these pilots, maybe we should take a look at ourselves.

Do we run through *life* with our own personal fuel supply dangerously low?

Not enough sleep?

Not enough exercise?

Right now, are we so completely engaged in the business of *business,* working so hard at *work,* that we're near the end of our emotional rope?

If the kids or the spouse or the boss seems to be grinding down what's left of our frayed nerves, perhaps it's because we're trying to stretch our fuel supply.

A good nap, a good book, lunch with a friend, personal quiet time—these can be valuable, even lifesaving, fuel stops.

With so many pressures on us these days it's essential that we take time to replenish our energy reserves.

When airplanes or people attempt to run on empty, the result is predictable.

Schooling—And Education

**One of the best historians
I ever knew never finished
the eighth grade.**

He had never attended high school. But five minutes of discussing world history with this man, and you knew he understood the great historical movements. In Africa. In Asia. In Europe.

He was one of the most interesting people I'd ever met because he was *interested.* His profound knowledge of the past was much more than a simple recitation of memorized dates. He knew the facts of history, but he also knew them in context.

How could he be such a storehouse of knowledge? I asked his son. The answer: Because he'd spent his entire life reading. Any book he could get his hands on—from the Old Testament to Toynbee. The man knew history because he loved it.

Over my years as a journalist, I've met many truly educated people who've lacked so-called *formal* education—people who were self-taught.

There was Eric Hoffer, the longshoreman-turned-philosopher. Hoffer's brilliant mind was educated on the docks, where he loaded freighters, and in libraries, where he spent his leisure time loading up his brain with the subjects he enjoyed.

When Bob Bray was a child, his family struggled to survive in a three-bedroom shack. They were so poor their house had no plumbing. Bray recalls how he hated the chore of heating the bathwater on the kitchen stove and going to the outdoor toilet during cold winters.

But through it all he nurtured his private dreams. They were incredibly big dreams for someone of such humble circumstances:

Dreams of having lunch with Bertrand Russell and Dame Edith Sitwell.

Dreams of wearing a cape like his hero, Frank Lloyd Wright.

How did such an impoverished boy even know about these famous people? What was the source of these dreams?

Despite their lack of money and education, Bray's mother and brother were avid readers. "We had books in every corner, on every surface, under anything on legs," Bray recalls.

Long before any formal schooling in interior design, long before he had become one of the world's most renowned interior designers, Bob Bray had begun his education.

Not everyone can go to college.

But *anyone* can be educated.

Making the Best of It

**Here's *one* thing you can
always plan on: Life won't always
go according to plan!**

When Chuck Colson signed on as one of President
Nixon's closest advisers, he certainly didn't expect to
end up in prison.

There's no way Colson could have foreseen how the web of
Watergate lies and deceit eventually would ensnare him, dramatically short-circuiting his high-powered career, ultimately
dashing his dreams and ambitions.

Chuck Colson might have lived out the rest of his life in
shame, despair and obscurity.

Instead he took his failures, his mistakes and his wrongdo-
ing and learned from them. He literally turned his life around.
Colson made a life-changing decision while in prison, and
when he was released, he dedicated the rest of his life to helping others who had stumbled.

He established Prison Ministries, leading that organization
with the kind of insight and compassion only a former convict

could possess. Those who've followed Chuck Colson's quiet but effective work recognize his sincerity. His commitments grow out of where he's been.

We all make mistakes. They may not be as big or as well publicized as Chuck Colson's. They probably won't have prison sentences attached.

But in ways big or small, we all mess up. We get off track. We fail.

Sometimes things simply don't turn out the way we'd planned. And sometimes we recognize that it *is* our fault.

Art Linkletter said by the time he'd reached the age of 60, life had taught him this lesson:

Things turn out best for people who make the best of the way things turn out.

A One-Way Street

**Is life real or is it Memorex?
What if we could rewind
and start all over?**

When I first started in the television business, videotape didn't exist. Everything was shot on film. It was limiting, and it was costly because once you'd shot something, it was permanently recorded. There was no chance to rewind and start over as we so easily do with tape.

Don't we sometimes wish life were like videotape? That if we didn't like a decision we'd made last year or a remark that had slipped out of our mouth last week, we could simply rewind and *take it from the top?*

The fact is life's like a film. Once the image is recorded, it's there for keeps. No rewinding. No backing up. No erasing. No starting over.

This reality doesn't have to be discouraging. Once we grasp that this is simply how it is, then we start to understand that what really counts is what's ahead.

Past mistakes are only important if we allow them to interfere with our future.

Lost opportunities are only an impediment if we dwell on them, letting them blind us to doors that are open right now.

Life becomes not only easier, but simpler once we accept that it's a one-way street.

No matter what route we've taken, or how many detours, there's no going back. There's only the road ahead, with its unmapped intersections and unanticipated adventures.

So, because there's no possible way to turn back, regrets are useless baggage.

Since life comes equipped only with a *forward* button, why waste time looking for the *rewind?*

"Look What I Found"

How difficult is it
to find *honesty* these days?
Can we trust people?

The story was datelined Franklin Park, Illinois. It was one of those small human-interest paragraphs. No big head-lines to grab attention. But surrounded by the day's dismal diary of police blotter journalism, this brief report stood out:

Mail carrier LaMonica Lewis had opened a drop box and discovered a bag intended for the bank. That bag contained $16,000, mostly in cash. Ms. Lewis had then taken it straight to the bank and said, "Look what I found!"

Unusual? Not typical of most people? Or has our cynical era become jaded to the good side of people by a barrage of news reports about crooks and cheaters?

Allow me some case studies for the defense of human nature:

Two summers ago at a major outdoor convention my wife left her purse on a bench. Within an hour someone had turned it in to lost and found. Everything was still in it, including the cash. Whoever turned it in didn't stick around for a reward or even a thank-you.

The day before I was to leave for an assignment in Eastern Europe, I lost my wallet on a busy street in Detroit. That wallet contained my passport, visa, credit cards and cash for the trip. That evening a man called to tell me he had found my wallet. When I retrieved it at his home, he refused any kind of payment. "It was the right thing to do," he explained.

A few months ago an acquaintance of ours lost her checkbook in Nashville. Within a week the checkbook showed up in the mail—anonymously. All of her checks as well as the credit cards that she'd tucked inside were still there.

Honesty, decency and trustworthiness are demonstrated, daily, in the lives of people all around us.

It's because these qualities are so normal—so expected— that they rarely get reported.

And *that's* the *good news!*

Corny? Or *Truthful?*

**Newer isn't always better.
Our craving for novelty may cost
us more than it's worth.**

Obsolescence keeps America's factories running and American workers working.

If light bulbs, toothbrushes and cars lasted a lifetime, the folks who make them would soon be out of business.

Dresses. Neckties. Music. Cars. New creations quickly make earlier ones look or sound old. Dated. Obsolete.

In the world of commerce such obsolescence—planned or otherwise—creates jobs.

But in the world of basic ideas obsolescence *can* create chaos.

Some ideas, of course, ought to change. New knowledge demands that we update our thinking.

However, when we discard perfectly good, time-tested *concepts* and *principles*—such as thoughtfulness, truthfulness, responsibility to our neighbors and to our community —when we brand these no longer useful because they're *outdated,* then our lives simply don't function as smoothly and society doesn't work as well.

Some truths don't come with expiration dates. Some *values* should never go out of style.

Generosity, loyalty, self-discipline, courage—these didn't come from a designer's drawing board only to be replaced by new, more fashionable concepts.

Sometimes such qualities seem quaint and corny to a society conditioned to demand the latest, the newest, the most up-to-date of everything, including ideas.

When someone suggested to Irving Berlin that his music was corny, he responded, "There is an element of truth in every idea that lasts long enough to be called corny."

It's the Process

**If we don't slow down
once in a while, nothing worthwhile
can catch up with us.**

We'd driven down the same street countless times.

Today we decided to walk. It was amazing how many things we saw that we had never noticed from the car.

Trees. Flowers. Shrubbery. The color and texture of houses. Details came into focus that had been little more than a blur as we would rush past in our car, always hurrying to get somewhere.

Today the goal was simply to enjoy the process of walking.

Often we're so focused on reaching a destination that we not only fail to *smell* the roses, we don't even *see* them.

A man I know, Tommy Bragg, meticulously restores antique furniture. He carefully repairs damaged finishes, replaces torn fabrics and then sometimes gives away to friends what he's spent weeks creating.

"I just enjoy doing it," he told me. "It's the *process* of making something beautiful that brings me pleasure."

My favorite relaxation is bass fishing. I rarely keep what I catch. I "thank" the fish for being a good sport and then gently drop him back into the water. This catch-and-release system works well for both me and the fish since it's the *process* of fishing I enjoy.

The process is far more important than the results. The calming effect of drifting lazily across smooth waters. Sharing fresh air and trees and sky with the infinite variety of birds that reside on our lake. The solitude. The break from disruptions and deadlines. The process. That's what it's all about.

"How's the fishing?" a neighbor called from shore as my boat motored slowly past his backyard.

"Fishing's great," I yelled back. "Catching's not so good today. But the fishing's *always* great."

A Most Potent Force

"Sticks and stones may break my
bones, but words can never hurt me!"
Don't you believe it.

D on't ever underestimate the power of words. Properly used, they can stir an entire nation into action.

Misunderstood . . . well . . .

It had been only two weeks since the assassination of Egypt's President Sadat.

My producer, Harvey Ovshinsky, and I were in Cairo, videotaping a documentary.

We'd failed in our attempts to arrange an interview with the new president, Hosni Mubarak. That was the bad news. The good news was, it seemed certain we'd be able to tape an interview with Sadat's widow the following day.

Harvey telephoned this information back to our news desk. In typical TV-news jargon, he announced, "Well, we missed our chance to get Mubarak today, but I think we've got a good shot at Mrs. Sadat tomorrow."

Clearly, "get Mubarak" and "a shot at Mrs. Sadat" had different meanings to a TV producer than to Egyptian security. Within seconds our phone went dead, and we had some serious explaining to do to nervous authorities who had been monitoring our conversations.

And if the meanings of words change depending upon who's speaking them, they can become even more confusing when translated into different languages:

Consider the Japanese hotel trying to be extremely hospitable to foreign guests. Their sign, translated into English, came out: *You are invited to take advantage of the chambermaid.*

In Rome an obstetrician proudly proclaimed that he specialized in *women and other diseases.*

Words, for good or for ill, are among the most potent forces known to humankind.

We're told a picture is worth a thousand words.

But I can show you words that are worth a thousand pictures: the Gettysburg Address. The Bill of Rights. The Sermon on the Mount. No mere picture could ever convey the feeling or the profound truths of these great words, so masterfully put together.

"Talk About a Minute"

**When you really have nothing
to say, then don't say it. Silence *is*
golden. It shouldn't be *rare*.**

We all admire the polished public speaker who, like Winston Churchill, can mobilize language and send it into battle.

But there's another kind of communicator who merits our respect: the one who says nothing. The one who can convey more with a look, a touch or a smile than most people can with a page full of words.

After the tragic death of a friend's daughter I told her grieving parents, "It's so difficult to find words at a time like this." But as the mother clutched my arm in silence, I realized words weren't necessary. *Being* there was what mattered.

When I was going through a period of personal grief a few years ago, a close friend dropped into my office, put his arm around me and just stood there silently for a moment. Then he left. Without a word he had communicated his care and his understanding. No words could have carried more comfort in that dark moment of my life.

Silent communication doesn't come easily for some of us. Especially those of us who talk for a living. Keeping our mouths shut is a skill we have to learn.

In Chicago, after an interminably long day of conferencing, the final speaker stepped to the podium.

"Folks, I think we've just about covered everything. If someone will suggest what they'd like me to talk about, I'd appreciate it."

And from the back of the room a voice responded:

"Talk about a minute."

Sometimes even *that's* too long.

A Million Dollars in California Oil

**Few things foul us up quicker
than bad information.
It always pays to get the *facts* first.**

It's impossible to reach good conclusions with bad
information.

The best military leaders and the best business executives
demand the most complete and accurate information available
before making a decision.

Hasty decisions often end up as disasters precisely because
they're made before all the facts are in.

World War Two historians generally agree that Hitler's
defeat in Russia resulted from poor information about both
Russian winters and Russian resolve.

Good bosses spend a lot of time gathering *information*
before coming down on an employee.

Good parents wait until they have the full story before dis-
ciplining their children.

Some of our most serious mistakes and profound apologies

occur because we speak or act based upon erroneous information.

An entrepreneur was introduced at a banquet as one of the most gifted businessmen in the nation. This was evidenced, the emcee said, by the fact that the man had made a million dollars in California oil.

When he got up to speak, the guest of honor seemed a bit embarrassed. He said the introduction was essentially correct.

Except that it wasn't oil, it was coal.

And it wasn't California, it was Pennsylvania.

And it wasn't a million, it was a hundred thousand dollars.

And it wasn't him, it was his brother.

And he didn't make it, he lost it.

Other than that the introduction was absolutely factual.

You know, we're all entitled to our own opinions.

But *none* of us can afford to be wrong in our *facts*.

Can You Afford It?

According to Woody Allen, money is better than poverty, if only for financial reasons.

M y colleague was staying at an expensive beach resort in the Caribbean. His postcard said: "Having a wonderful time; wish I could afford it."

The truth is this guy has so much money he doesn't even know his son's in college.

Not because he earns a super income. It's because he manages his personal checkbook with the efficiency of a successful business.

He's learned a most basic truth: You really don't have a wonderful time when you can't afford it. If a person's got more money than brains, be assured it's a temporary condition.

Millions of Americans right now are sinking deeper and deeper into the quicksand of credit cards and irresponsible spending. Are people actually putting American Express balances on their MasterCard card? Yes.

The problem of personal debt has proliferated so much that it's created a whole new industry: credit counseling.

But you don't need a seminar to understand the bottom line. It's simply: Don't spend more than you make.

It's true whether you push a lawnmower for minimum wage or run a Fortune 500 corporation.

This is much more than an economic issue. Money mismanagement destroys marriages, wrecks family relationships, ruins self-esteem and sabotages careers.

And budgets do work: I know one young couple who insist they're saving an incredible amount on entertainment since adopting a budget.

Here's how it works: By the time they write down their expenses and balance everything each day, it's too late to go out.

Pulp *Non*fiction

**There are organizations to
help people with *drug* addictions.
What do they have for us *data* junkies?**

O ur bedroom might be mistaken for a doctor's waiting room except that *our* periodicals are current.

Long ago they ceased to fit inside any production-model magazine rack. Now they overflow tub-like baskets Renee bought in a desperate move to contain them.

The printed word can be found on, around and under virtually every piece of bedroom furniture. In one corner a stack of newspapers serves as sort of coffee table holding up three piles of magazines.

Renee says if they ever do a movie called Pulp *Non*fiction, it should be filmed on location—in our bedroom.

Once, in the middle of the night, I stepped out of bed and squarely onto a short stack of *Newsweek*s. It was like hitting a patch of ice, and before you could say *"Time,"* I was flat on the floor somewhere between the *Wall Street Journal* and *USA Today.*

It can be argued that, as a writer, I require more than the normal number of publications. I know it can be argued because I've argued it many times. To which Renee responds with disgusting logic: "Ridiculous."

This year I'm determined to get a handle on my subscription addiction. Exercise some self-discipline at renewal time. "Read my lips," I pledge to Renee. "I just wish you'd read your magazines," she retorts.

Some people worry that fires, floods, hurricanes or termites will destroy their home.

These just may be the only hope of *saving* ours.

The Best Medicine

**If you ever say
"I'm so mad I could die,"
you just may be right!**

Medical evidence that anger can kill us continues to mount.

Hostility may damage the human heart as much as smoking.

One study shows people prone to temper tantrums are *twice* as likely to die from heart disease.

But what can a person who has a short fuse do? Aren't hot tempers genetic?

I remember a friend in high school who had a hair-trigger temper. When he got drafted, his mother worried that he'd be court-martialed before he finished basic training.

But a funny thing happened. Somehow my friend learned rather quickly how to restrain his temper. Looking back now as a military veteran, this doesn't surprise me. From my own experience, I learned that drill sergeants have a way of helping young hotheads get control of their *uncontrollable* tempers.

Fortunately there are ways to neutralize hostility without joining the army. One of the best is learning to laugh.

As a journalist I've frequently watched anger disarmed by a quip. I've seen stalled labor negotiations nudged back on track because someone broke the tension with a joke.

What's good for society in general can be terrific for individuals in particular because if anger kills, laughter heals.

If you've read his book *Anatomy of an Illness,* you know that Norman Cousins overcame a life-threatening illness by watching old Marx Brothers movies. For Cousins, laughter may have been not only the best medicine, but the only effective one.

Is it purely coincidence that so many comedians have lived well into their 80s and 90s?

Henny Youngman.

Milton Berle.

Bob Hope.

Red Skelton.

George Burns.

If there were a *fountain of youth,* I suspect it would spring from the deep, refreshing wells of humor, which may add years to our lives.

Certainly they add life to our years.

Lighten Up!

**If you want to be taken seriously,
laugh at yourself.**

Harry Reasoner once said he never trusted any organization that couldn't find something about itself to laugh at.

Organizations and individuals accomplish more when they take their *goals* seriously but not *themselves.*

When you're watching one of the daytime shout shows on TV, don't you sometimes want to talk back to the screen and say "Hey, folks, lighten up"?

The issues may be quite serious: crime, health care, child abuse, assisted suicide—but yelling doesn't improve understanding, and being *uptight* doesn't advance any cause.

Maybe it wouldn't be as entertaining, but wouldn't it be more productive to have less confrontation and more communication? Less arrogance, more humility?

Wouldn't you like to hear the zealots for any cause concede just once that maybe they don't have all the answers? That perhaps there is a *legitimate* other point of view?

Children are naturally better than adults at approaching

ponderous issues with a light touch. Consider this essay a fourth-grade girl wrote to define human differences:

"People," she stated, "are composed of girls and boys. Also men and women. Boys are no good at all until they grow up and get married.

"Men who do not get married are no good either. Boys are an awful bother. My mother is a woman, and my father is a man. A woman is a grown-up girl with children. My father is such a nice man that I think he must have been a girl when he was a boy."

"Start by Creating a Universe"

Whatever happened to the self-made man (or woman)?

A friend complained the other day that there just aren't any self-made men like the ones who first developed this nation.

Where, she wanted to know, are the Henry Fords, the Thomas Edisons, the Andrew Carnegies—men who began with nothing and climbed their way to the top of the ladder. In some instances even creating the ladder.

It should not take away from their considerable accomplishments to suggest that there is no such thing as a *self-made* man. Or woman.

When Dr. Benjamin Hooks was honored for his work with the NAACP, he responded:

"You know, friends, whenever I see a turtle sitting up on top of a fence post, I know he didn't get there by himself."

People who boast that they're *self-made* overlook a lot of help they've received on the way up.

Every friend, every institution, every book and article that inspires, nurtures, encourages or critiques—each shares credit for whatever we ultimately make of ourselves.

The late Carl Sagan once said if you really want to bake an apple pie from scratch, you'll have to start by creating a universe.

So what did happen to the self-made man of American folklore? The truth is, he never really existed. He's as much a figment of the imagination as the Loch Ness monster.

The beginning of true independence is recognizing our *inter*dependence.

Self-made people exist only in their own minds.

And egos.

Quality Counts

**What is the winning edge
that distinguishes *champions* from
those who are *merely good?***

Excellence used to be one of our core values.

Teachers taught it. Parents encouraged it.

Skilled craftsmen practiced it, often raising a trade to the level of an art.

Somewhere between the *Industrial Revolution* and the *Information Age* it seems we lowered our aim.

We compromised quality in the name of efficiency.

For growing numbers of us *average* became an acceptable goal. Just *getting by* was okay. Being good enough was *good enough.*

Then we Americans got a brutal wake-up call in the form of a double whammy: the rapid acceleration of automation and increased international competition for jobs.

Suddenly it seemed both the Japanese and the Europeans were outperforming us in efficiency *and* quality. Improved foreign productivity increased pressure on U.S. industries to do more with fewer people.

As competition for jobs intensified, we began to rediscover that *quality* counts. We began to understand that in today's world excellence can determine not only success but *survival!*

In a recent speed-skating competition Bonnie Blair won in 36.3 seconds. The skater who finished 22nd came in at 36.8. *First place and 22nd place were separated by only one-half second.*

The difference between good and best can be razor thin.

Inspiring our children to be *the best* is to prepare them for a future where opportunities will expand even as the margin between success and failure continues to shrink.

Any Old Mule Can Kick Down a Barn

Which would *you* find the most fun: creating, or just creating havoc?

Across the street from my office they demolished a tall building. In less than a week the entire brick and steel structure was nothing but a pile of dusty rubble.

I don't know how long it took to construct the building. But one wrecker's ball and a couple of bulldozers had *un*done in days what must have required months or years of skilled labor to *do*.

Watching the operation, I wondered whether the demolition crew got as much satisfaction from destroying it as the builders must have gotten from creating it.

It's not likely, because there's something in most people that responds more positively to building up than to tearing down. There's a saying that any old mule can kick down a barn, but it takes a skilled carpenter to build one.

Most of us like beginnings better than endings. Christenings and bar mitzvahs are better than funerals.

We'd rather receive a wedding announcement than word

that a good friend is getting divorced.

Nevertheless some people do seem to derive more pleasure from tearing down a reputation than from passing on a compliment; from hammering away at faults than from offering encouragement. It's usually advisable to ignore such people.

A young musician was feeling terrible because his concert had been badly mauled by the critics. Famed composer Sibelius patted him gently on the shoulder and said, "Remember, son, there is no city anywhere in the world where they've erected a statue of a critic."

A Sign of True Talent

**Learning to forget is one
of life's most valuable lessons. A *bad*
memory can be a *good* thing!**

They say an elephant never forgets.

If that's true, then elephants must be miserable animals because it's impossible to be happy while remembering everything.

Every argument you've ever had with your spouse.

Every disagreement with your children.

Every insult or indignity you've received at work or at a store.

I've always admired people with so-called photographic memories. The ability to recall a name, a face, an incident— this can be good in business or professional relationships. It can be critical for an actor, required to commit lengthy scripts to memory.

But there are times—many times—when we're happier— *and healthier*—if we allow ourselves to forget.

Nothing eats us up inside like a lingering, festering grudge.

Resentment is an emotional acid, destroying *first* the container that holds it.

People who are truly successful at living are magnanimous. They're big enough to let go of slights and indignities. They're too busy building the future to waste time on wrongs from the past. They don't get hung up on the desire for revenge.

The ability to remember is a sign of true talent.

But the ability to forget—*that* can be the mark of true greatness.

The Home-Field Advantage

**Cheering doesn't win games.
But cheering may provide
the winning margin!**

Every sports fan knows about the *home-field advantage.*

Sometimes enthusiastic cheering from the bleachers can provide the margin between failure and success.

It's true in athletics.

It's true in life.

I once interviewed a young college graduate from a rather poor family who told me how his mother's encouragement and enthusiasm for education were all that kept him from dropping out of school.

Tears trickled down the mother's cheeks as her son explained that he was the first member of his family ever to complete college. Without Mom's cheerleading, he wouldn't have stuck it out.

In the early 1980s I was one of several journalists invited to the White House for lunch with President Ronald Reagan.

The most vivid impression of the man I took away was of his contagious enthusiasm and his great skill at motivating people.

Whether you agreed with his politics or not, you had to concede that President Reagan knew how to inspire Americans to believe they could *be* better, *do* better and *go further.*

Winning in sports or in life takes discipline, dedication and perseverance. It also requires strong belief in possibilities. That belief can be renewed and reinforced each time we hear encouraging applause from the sidelines of our lives.

Watching him each evening on ABC's *Nightline,* most viewers are unaware that my old friend and colleague, Ted Koppel, once took a leave of absence from the network to become a househusband. Ted took care of the children and the home while his wife, Grace Ann, finished law school. Ted was her biggest cheerleader.

Sometimes we play the game.

Sometimes we sit on the sidelines.

But all of us—all the time—can be cheerleaders for those looking to us for that home court advantage.

Welcome It As a Friend

**Criticism is like pain.
We don't like it.
But it may serve a useful purpose.**

If you don't want to be criticized, then don't do anything. Of course that's no guarantee. Someone is sure to criticize you then for being lazy or lacking ambition.

Actually it's impossible to avoid criticism, so we might as well develop a strategy for dealing with it.

First it's important to sort criticism into two categories: fair and unfair.

Constructive criticism may help us grow, develop and improve. That kind we should welcome as a friend.

It's the other kind that's most difficult to handle. Unfair criticism. Distorted diatribes not only false, but sometimes maliciously motivated.

Such criticism may be as private as gossip at the office or as public as a front-page headline.

In Boston a man had been severely, and he believed, unfairly, criticized by the local paper. The attack was so scathing that he was considering a lawsuit. At the very least he would demand a public apology.

His good friend listened as the man indignantly outlined what he might do. Finally he cooled off enough to ask his friend, "What do *you* think?"

The friend replied, "I'd suggest you do nothing. You see, half the people who read that paper never saw the article about you. Half of those who read it don't understand it. Half of those who understand it don't believe it. And half of those who believe it aren't of any consequence."

It's always healthy to put criticism into perspective.

And to remember the sage observation of Walter Winchell: "Nobody will ever get ahead of you as long as he's kicking you in the seat of the pants."

The Value of Daydreaming

**If you're ever accused of imagining
things, take it as a compliment.
Not everyone can do it!**

As I was growing up, my parents provided me with many things for which I'm grateful: love, faith, security and the desire to pursue excellence.

But among their greatest gifts was an appreciation of fantasy. My parents understood the value of daydreaming. Of imagination. Of wishful thinking.

When I was four, I had a cadre of imaginary friends. To this day I can remember two of their names—Ollie and Doc. They went with me everywhere.

One time as Mother and I had just entered a store, I told her, "You shut the door too soon. You slammed it on Doc, and he's still outside."

Instead of trying to explain that Doc was only a figment of a child's imagination, Mother dutifully walked back, opened the door and held it long enough for my make-believe friend to join us.

One evening she gave Ollie and Doc imaginary baths when I insisted that if I had to get clean, they should, too.

Little did I understand at the time what a heritage my parents were providing.

I was too young to comprehend that every accomplishment in life begins with a thought—that the more we can imagine, the more we can do.

The car we drive, the clothes we wear, the house or apartment we live in—each began as a desire, and a desire begins as a *thought.*

The hand can achieve only what the mind has first conceived.

Great buildings, great corporations, great music, literature, art and scientific discoveries all began as somebody's thought.

And it isn't only *great* things that start with the imagination. It's all things, big and small.

That's why dreamers should be encouraged.

Often.

And early.

"Do Something Good for Somebody"

The unhappiest people in the world are those who go through life with a catcher's mitt on both hands.

It's been said that *takers* may eat better, but *givers* sleep better.

Givers also seem to get along better emotionally.

Dr. Karl Menninger had completed a lecture on mental health. A medical student asked, "Dr. Menninger, if someone came to you feeling dejected and really down in the dumps, what would you prescribe?"

The renowned psychiatrist gave an answer that was neither clinical nor complicated:

"I would advise that person," he said, "to shut up the house, go across to the poor part of town and do something good for somebody."

Clearly this distinguished physician wasn't talking about clinical depressions. But Dr. Menninger did understand that a lot of personal despair comes from too much thinking about *ourselves* and too little concern for *others*.

It's easy to get into a cycle of self-centeredness. And it's fairly simple to break that cycle if we choose.

It's as basic as following Dr. Menninger's prescription: Do something good for someone. A good place to start might be a nearby nursing home. There's probably more loneliness per square foot in a nursing home than in any other building in the nation.

We have major organizations set up to fight cancer, heart disease, rheumatism and AIDS. For virtually every serious disease there's a group working on behalf of those afflicted.

But there is no American Loneliness Society. No Heartache Foundation of America.

Consider the numbers of people who suffer, chronically, from abandonment and neglect. It's not only the elderly. It's children. The divorced. Widows and widowers. Chronic invalids confined to their homes and, sometimes, living alone.

There's no national loneliness fund for the forgotten. Where are the research dollars to treat this devastating condition?

Fortunately loneliness responds quite well to the sincere efforts of nonprofessionals.

And there's a funny thing about helping others: It's almost impossible to do it without helping ourselves.

Don't take my word for it.

Ask Dr. Menninger.

Is He Working or Relaxing?

It's a lot easier to tell where the other person is going if we know where he's been.

It was a comprehension test for first graders.

The teacher had placed two pictures on the blackboard.

One showed a man chopping wood. The other, a man sitting in an easy chair, reading.

The teacher asked the class, "Which man is working, and which one is relaxing?"

To the teacher's surprise one little girl said the man chopping wood was relaxing while the one reading the book was working.

When the teacher asked her to explain, the child told her, "My dad's a professor. He reads when he works, and he chops wood for fun."

So much of what seem to be differences of *opinion* turn out to be differences of *viewpoint*. Differences created by our own personal histories and perspectives.

Fundamentally all humans have the same needs, desires, hopes and dreams. But our view of how best to meet those needs is shaped by all the forces and influences in our lives. And *those* are what make us seem so different.

A high school teacher in Kansas thought he'd help some of his city students understand a little more about country life. So he posed a math question: *If a cow gave so many quarts of milk a day, and the milk weighed so many pounds and averaged X percent butterfat, how many pounds of butterfat would she produce in a week?*

Half a dozen papers came up with the wrong answer. And to the teacher's puzzlement it was the *same* wrong answer. The teacher knew his kids hadn't been cheating.

Finally he figured it out. Those six youngsters with the wrong answer were all from the city. They'd all assumed the cow worked a five-day week.

You Carry It with You

How do we find security in an *in*secure world?

It was a graduate course in newswriting.

We were all journalism students, confident in the knowledge that networks and newspapers eagerly awaited our graduation.

We would be our generation's Ed Murrows, Walter Cronkites and Walter Lippmanns.

But our instructor, a veteran of the world that awaited us, tempered our confidence with a candid dose of reality:

"Let me assure you that the only security any of you will ever have is what you carry right here," he said as he pointed to his head.

Professor Baskett Moss was sharing one of life's most important truths: that security never comes from contracts or employment agreements. It comes from ability, skill and dedication. He was telling us that for journalists, job security had to come from within.

Today in every career field Professor Moss's observation is becoming more relevant. Computerization, automation and corporate downsizing underscore the reality that security is something we have to carry around in our own heads.

When we feel secure about ourselves and in our abilities, external uncertainties can serve as important motivators. When Sherwood Anderson first started his career as a writer, his publisher thought he'd help out by sending Sherwood a check every Friday. Not a lot. Just enough money to meet expenses.

But after three weeks Sherwood Anderson couldn't stand it any longer. He carried the check back to the publisher, unopened, and said:

"It's no use. It's just impossible for me to write with *security* staring me in the face."

"I Have Never Been in Any Accident"

Vigilance is the price of freedom. But keeping our head up and our eyes open can buy us a lot more than that!

When I was a teenager, I wrecked my very first car during a single moment of inattention.

It was raining and foggy. I glanced down briefly to tune the radio, but that careless moment was long enough for me to ram into an abandoned car stalled on the road ahead of me.

Fortunately my injuries were not critical. But sometimes even the *briefest* lapse in attention can create tragedies that last a lifetime.

One thoughtless word can destroy a friendship.

One careless act can destroy a future.

To succeed, or even to survive, these days demands unending attention to detail.

Complacency can sabotage marriages, jobs or health.

Ironically the longer we survive *without* a disaster, the more vulnerable we become to smugness and apathy.

Consider these words written by a veteran sea captain:

"When anyone asks me how I can best describe my experience in nearly 40 years at sea, I merely say, 'Uneventful.'

"In all my experience, I have never been in any accident...

"I have seen but one vessel in distress in all my years at sea.

"I never saw a wreck and never have been wrecked, nor was I ever in any predicament that threatened to end in disaster of any sort."

Those words were written in 1907 by E. J. Smith.

Captain of the *Titanic*.

The Gift of Today

Where do *you* think is the very best place to live?

We were on a business trip in Scottsdale, Arizona.

The sky was clear blue.

The air was dry, and the sun urged us to remove our jackets.

The day was, in a word, perfect.

As we headed for the airport and a flight back to our snowy Great Lakes home, Renee smiled and said, "Makes you wonder why anybody chooses to live with our winters, doesn't it?"

Of course we can't all live in the Sunbelt. Nor would all of us want to. Jobs, family or a genuine love of the changing seasons all influence where we live geographically.

But we can *always* choose where to live emotionally. And the best place to live is *right now.* This moment.

Yet we waste so many of our present moments trying to live in the past.

Agonizing over past mistakes.

Sifting through all the "I should's" and "Why didn't I's" that really don't matter because all the regrets in the world can't recapture the past. It's over.

We also squander many of our *nows*, trying to live in the future. Anticipating all the terrible things that might happen. Tormenting ourselves with gloomy anxieties or teasing ourselves with wishful thinking.

It can be instructive to learn from the past and inspiring to build for the future.

But the fact is that both the road behind us and the road ahead of us are nonexistent.

Yesterday is history.

Tomorrow is a promise.

Today is a gift. Maybe that's why it's called *the present.*

And there is no better place to live!

Go Ahead, Make Their Day

**When people act *un*reasonably,
often there *is* a reason. But it
doesn't always show.**

It was near closing time when I showed up at the counter. The clerk did not try to hide her irritation.

I felt like pointing to the clock and reminding her that the store was open for another seven minutes. Instead I apologized for running in at the last minute and told her I hoped it didn't cause her to be late for whatever she had going on after work.

Recognizing that I had picked up on her frustration, she responded, "Actually I should apologize to you. It's just that my mother was taken to the hospital today. I'm really worried about her, and I'm going to see her just as soon as I get off work."

Then she added, "Thanks for being so understanding."

Everybody we meet is dealing with something. No matter how calm, serene or happy we appear, we're all struggling.

One afternoon I stopped by the office of a woman who had been working extraordinarily hard for our company. She was quite intense, laboring over her word processor, when I said, "Don't want to interrupt, but just wanted you to know you're doing a great job. I appreciate you."

Her face brightened.

"Mort, you've made my day," she said.

And it had been so easy. It didn't cost me anything to pass along that genuine compliment. But in a world where criticism is abundant and praise is scarce, it had meant a lot to her.

So if someone seems surly or abrupt today—a clerk, a boss, a spouse—imagine what they may be dealing with.

Then go ahead, make their day.

Mine Eyes Have Seen the Glory . . .

**If the music's gone sour
and you can't change the tune,
change the lyrics!**

W here music is concerned, life truly does imitate art. Sometimes our days resound like a symphony of joy.

Sometimes they echo like a funeral dirge.

Maybe the hopeful strains of "Here Comes the Bride" have degenerated into "Here Come the Lawyers."

Possibly the merry melody "Off to Work We Go" has become a discordant "Take This Job and Shove It."

Perhaps the sweet lullaby of innocent childhood has given way to the raucous sounds of rebellious teenagers.

What do we do when the music goes bad?

If we can't change the tune, maybe we *can* change the lyrics.

Few songs are more uplifting than "The Battle Hymn of the Republic." When Abraham Lincoln heard it for the first time, he wept.

But that tune wasn't always accompanied by such moving words. Originally the song was a bawdy ballad sung lustily by

Union troops on their way to the Southern battle zone. You've probably heard those earlier lyrics—in "John Brown's Body."

Julia Ward Howe recognized in that tune the potential for something more. In her mind she heard different words. And in substituting those immortal lines, "Mine eyes have seen the glory of the coming of the Lord," she converted that earthy ballad into an inspiring masterpiece.

What music life will produce isn't always our call.

But more often than we might think, we can rewrite the lyrics.

A Quality Within

Is there anyone, anywhere who can make you happy? It's not likely!

There is *no one* who can make you or me happy.

That's because *happiness* isn't something that's done to us or for us. It's a quality we either find within ourselves or don't find at all.

Certainly there are people who can provide us with companionship. Friendship. Diversion. Pleasure. Even love. But happiness? Fortunately, that's entirely up to us.

Fortunately, because when anyone says to someone else, "I just can't be happy without you," that person has voluntarily surrendered control of a most important part of life.

We're constructed emotionally so that our happiness does not have to depend upon another person. That's a good thing because dependency not only is psychologically damaging, it can be dangerous.

Take the case of the man who'd gone to the doctor for a physical exam. After the doctor completed his work, he pulled the wife aside and said, "Madam, unless you do the following, your husband isn't going to be around too long."

The doctor then prescribed what the wife was to do:

"Every morning be certain he gets a good, healthy breakfast.

"Have him come home for lunch every day so you can feed him a low-fat, high-fiber, balanced meal.

"Make sure you serve him a hot dinner every night and don't burden him with household chores.

"Also," the doctor continued, "keep the house spotless so he's never exposed to any unnecessary germs."

Later, on their way home, the husband asked his wife what the doctor had said.

She paused for a moment. Then she replied, "Honey, the doctor thinks you're going to die!"

"Now, Do I Tell My Partner?"

Everybody's *talking* about ethics.
What are we *doing* about it?

When Michael Sovern announced his resignation as president of Columbia University, he told a reporter he was leaving with only one major regret: that *ethics* wasn't being taught in universities.

He conceded that the professional schools—law, medicine, journalism—have some pretty good programs in *professional* ethics. But the average undergraduate gets no training in basic values.

Sovern's concern is underscored by a two-year study conducted for the Josephson Institute. It found that nearly 2 out of 10 college students admitted to shoplifting within the past year. And more than 3 out of 10 admitted to cheating on at least one exam.

This survey included students from private and religious schools. Most came from middle- and upper-middle-income families.

While it would be unfair to dump all the blame on parents,

it is fair to assume many youngsters are not getting the right ethical messages at home.

One high school girl went to her father for help with a term paper assignment on ethics and asked, "Just what is ethics?"

Her dad owned a dry cleaning shop, and he told her that he had faced an ethical question that very day. He had found a $100 bill in the pocket of a customer's coat.

"Now," he explained, "the ethical question is this: Do I tell my partner?"

Thinking About the Next Guy

Why is it that some coaches with good players still can't win games?

What makes a winning team?

Never forgetting fundamentals, for one thing.

But there's more:

Legendary football coach Vince Lombardi believed that the primary requirement is teamwork.

He believed that teamwork spells the difference between mediocrity and greatness.

"Each player has to be thinking about the next guy," Lombardi said.

"They've got to *care* for one another."

Mountain climbers certainly understand the importance of such teamwork.

In 1953 Sir Edmund Hillary and his guide became the first humans ever to reach the top of Mount Everest.

On their way down Hillary slipped and started to fall. He most certainly would have been killed if his guide hadn't immediately dug in his ice ax and, at great risk to himself, braced the rope linking the two men together.

When they reached the base of the mountain, news reporters made a big deal out of the guide's heroism. But he brushed it off with a simple response:

"Mountain climbers always help each other."

Each autumn I watch the geese cross our lake and head south for the winter. I remember reading once why they always fly in those familiar V-formations. As each bird flaps its wings, it creates an uplift for the bird immediately following.

Scientists claim that by flying in the V-formation the flock adds at least 71 percent greater range than if each bird flew by itself.

When it comes to teamwork, you'd think we humans would have at least as much sense as a *goose.*

"This Really *Is* Important"

**What's a priority is all in the mind of
the person doing the *prioritizing!***

Only *you* know what's most important to *you.*

"Some of my friends can't understand why I drive an old clunker of a car and live in a neighborhood that's not as nice as theirs," the man told me.

"But those things just aren't important to me. I'm happy with my life. I do what I want to do, and I don't have a lot of the stress many of my friends have," he said.

Whatever we value, it's a very personal choice and one we shouldn't have to justify to anyone.

Before leaving for a news assignment in Egypt a few years ago, we asked my mother to stay with our children. We left telephone numbers and told our son, Al, who was in high school, to call if there were any emergencies.

You can imagine our concern when the telephone rang in our hotel room near the Great Pyramid at three in the morning and I heard his voice. I immediately wondered what terrible crisis had prompted the call.

First he apologized for having forgotten the time difference. But the call was urgent. In his mind, it bordered on an emergency.

"Sorry to call so late, Dad, but this really *is* important," he explained.

"The Rolling Stones are coming to town for a concert, and if I don't get my tickets today, all the best seats will be gone."

I suspect it wasn't Dad's permission he was looking for so much as it was for a financial commitment.

Clearly, on the issue of a Rolling Stones concert, Al and I did not share the same set of priorities.

Don't we *all* have different ideas of what's important?

There's a tombstone in Wisconsin that leaves no doubt about the priority of the deceased:

Under the man's name and the dates of his birth and death is carved this inscription: *Bowled 300 in 1982.*

Big Bogey

**Sometimes our personal
histories are written in diaries;
sometimes in the lives of our pets.**

He was a Christmas gift for our seven-year-old daughter,
Carey.

A stubby-legged miniature dachshund who never looked
into a mirror and always believed he was 10 feet tall.

Bogey could be a *brat,* chewing books and leaving his
unmistakable signature on carpets.

But he also could be charming, providing Carey a sympa-
thetic ear through adolescent crises and comfort when her
mother was ill. After Carey's mother died, Bogey was there
with unconditional love.

We hardly noticed, but while Carey was growing up, Bogey
was growing old.

Some mornings he could barely see and hardly move. Pain
was in his eyes. The day I first had to *carry* him outside, he
was unable to stand when I set him down.

Carey was half a continent away. When I called her to explain Bogey's condition and the decision that had to be made, she wept softly, but she understood. Understanding doesn't always make something hurt less.

The vet's needle had always provoked a yelp from Bogey. This time there wasn't even a whimper. As the drug began almost immediately to take effect, Bogey's pain was easing. Ours knotted in our throats. We stroked him gently until he was gone.

Today his ashes blend with clover and wildflowers on the peninsula where he often would run through grass taller than he, chasing ducks he could never catch.

One morning during a quiet walk along the lake, I was reflecting on the years of happiness this tiny dog had brought to our daughter.

In that moment I realized Bogey had been right all along.

He really *was* much bigger than he looked.

On Gratitude

They say familiarity breeds contempt. It may also breed *complacency!*

Happiness doesn't produce gratitude. It's the other way around.

People who are grateful *are* happy. Those who wait for something to happen so they can *be* grateful end up being neither grateful nor happy.

Gratitude is a paradox. Sometimes we think *What do I have to be grateful for?* But that thinking misses the most basic truth about gratitude: It produces its own reasons. When we practice the attitude of gratitude, we begin to recognize all kinds of good things for which we *should* be grateful.

I grew up in a home where a blessing was always said at the table. Mother was a terrific cook, but it wasn't her great meals that inspired the prayers. It was the genuine gratitude my parents felt for the food we ate. For the earth and sun and rain that produced it. For the farmers who tended and harvested it.

For the stores that packaged and sold it. They were grateful for the Creator they credited with life itself.

It was a home where no good thing was taken for granted. As children we were reminded that the very air which sustains life is a rare gift in a universe virtually devoid of such atmosphere. We were taught to be grateful for friends, family, school, work, health, freedom—even our own consciousness.

Circumstances do not create gratitude or ingratitude. That's why we can read of a Bosnian refugee expressing thanks just for being alive on the same day we hear ourselves complaining about something as trivial as being stuck in traffic.

Of all the useful lessons I learned as a child, none has proved more valuable than what my parents taught me about gratitude.

It's as simple as love.

As profound as happiness.

And as vital to life as the air we breathe.

"This Guy Will Be Trouble"

Books aren't the *only* things you can't judge by their covers.

"**B**et you can't guess what I got you," my daughter said excitedly as she handed me the birthday gift she'd wrapped herself.

The size and shape of the necktie box were a dead give-away. Naturally I didn't let on. What kind of dad would ruin a four-year-old's surprise?

While that package was obvious, others can be deceiving. You can't always tell by size and shape just what's inside.

Once at Christmastime I put a sweater and a *brick* in a box the size of a golf bag. It was a gift for our son, and one of his favorite activities was to pick up gifts from under the tree, shake them and try to determine what they were. *This* one fooled him completely.

People are like that. Sometimes their *packaging* is deceptive.

After Dick Smith retired from selling, he and Judy bought a bed-and-breakfast in St. Augustine, Florida.

This second career brought both of them new insights about people.

Dick told me about the bearded man in the leather jacket wearing chains and tattoos and roaring up on a Harley. Dick's first impression: *This guy will be nothing but trouble.*

Instead of being a Hell's Angel, he proved to be one of the nicest, most interesting gentlemen ever to check in at Dick and Judy's small hotel.

On the other hand, the sharply dressed, clean-shaven young man who looked like the class valedictorian turned out to be a common thief.

They caught *this* guest rummaging through the dresser drawers in their private quarters.

Dick told me, "Running that inn taught Judy and me that you really can't judge people by their clothes or the length of their hair."

He might have added you also can't judge them by the color of their skin, their accent or their religion.

What you *think* you see isn't necessarily what you get, for quality and character—like Christmas gifts—can come in a variety of packages.

Well-Adjusted and Funny

If life's a trip, laughter is the shock absorbers.

The average mom who works outside the home spends about 84 hours a week taking care of both jobs.

Magazine editor Karen Levine is one of those supermoms. When she feels overwhelmed, Karen recalls a birthday card her mother sent a few years ago.

On the cover are these words:

"My daughter, she's a wife, mother, worker, cook, house cleaner, chauffeur and volunteer."

Inside is the punch line:

"My daughter, she's a basket case."

During my career as a journalist, I've found humor in the newsroom to be an important emotional cushion against the traumas and tragedies we cover daily.

Doctors and nurses in emergency rooms, the clergy, police officers—all have discovered the serious, therapeutic role humor plays in helping them through harsh realities.

Some of the funniest stories are those that weren't intended to be humorous. For instance, the answers British children gave to a series of questions asked in church school:

One of them guessed that Noah's wife was called Joan of Ark.

Another wrote that Lot's wife was a pillar of salt by day and a ball of fire by night.

Still another reckoned that a Republican is a sinner mentioned in the Bible.

Actor Tom Hanks told a reporter he has two goals for his children: He wants them to be well-adjusted and funny.

That may be redundant. Today being well-adjusted—coping with the demands of daily living—demands a good sense of humor.

Deny It—Or at Least Discount It

When it comes to tabloid journalism, there's nothing so small that it can't be blown out of proportion.

When I was anchoring TV news in Philadelphia, a viewer told me she and her husband always wondered: "Should we watch your 6:00 news and get indigestion, or wait till 11:00 and get insomnia?"

Many viewers tell me they are alarmed and disgusted by the graphic depiction of violence, crime and sexual excesses.

Garrison Keillor says that sometimes you just have to look reality in the eye—and deny it!

Where TV is concerned, we may need to look reality in the eye—and discount it. Not that what's reported isn't true. It's just that it represents only part of the truth—mostly the *negative* part.

Of course there are people who rob banks, beat their children, cheat on their taxes or have kinky sex lives.

But the bad and the bizarre are not *typical* of real life for most of us most of the time.

Virtually every national survey shows *crime* the number-one concern of Americans. This despite the fact we're making progress against crime, with many classes of violent crimes actually on the decline.

Crime is the number-one *concern* because it's the number-one *news topic*.

In his stand-up routine, nightclub comic Wally Cox used to describe how he would buy a newspaper, take it home, put it in a drawer and leave it there for two weeks. Then, when he took it out, he'd read the headlines and say, "Thank God that's not happening today."

Unfortunately, live, *as-it-happens* news reports don't allow us time to develop such a healthy, long-term perspective.

Look Off to the Side

What we *see* isn't always what we *get.* To reach our goal we may need to be looking at something else.

It was an air force class for pilots and crew.

"Funny thing about flying at night," the instructor told us.

"To see the instruments most clearly, you don't want to stare directly at them. You have to look just slightly off to the side."

Not being an ophthalmologist, I didn't fully understand the physiology, and I still don't.

But as a civilian pilot who's logged a lot of night flying hours, I recognize that it's true.

It is also a metaphor for one of life's paradoxes:

Often we achieve *one* goal by aiming for *another.*

Take success. People who aim for success as a primary goal rarely achieve it. But those who attempt to do something extraordinarily well, frequently become successful in the process.

Erma Bombeck said, "Don't confuse fame with success. Madonna is one; Helen Keller is the other."

Albert Einstein, one of the 20th century's universally acknowledged successes, was asked, "Doctor, why are we here?"

Einstein turned to his questioner in surprise that he had asked so elementary a question.

He replied, "We are here to serve other people."

Examine the biographies of those historical figures we revere today as *great*. All earned that greatness by what they gave back to the world—in music, literature, philosophy, commerce, medicine.

Success is a by-product. It comes to those who are concentrating on some more important goal.

Like looking at aircraft instruments at night, you see it best when you don't stare directly at it.

Play Your Cards

**Caution: Worry can be hazardous
to your health. And besides,
it doesn't help.**

In his later years Mark Twain observed that he was an old
man who'd seen lots of troubles, "most of which never
happened."

How much energy is wasted on worry.

But it's more than a waste: It's a hazardous waste.

Dr. Charles Mayo claims that "Worry affects the circula-
tion, the heart, the glands, the whole nervous system." And
while he's never known people to die from overwork, he has
known them to die from worry.

So, how can we stop it?

Astronaut Jim Lovell knows the secret. I heard him reveal
it during a news conference where he was asked about *Apollo
13*. He was in command of that spacecraft when it experienced an explosion on its way to the moon.

With their oxygen almost gone, their electrical system out,
their spaceship plunging toward lunar orbit, it appeared

Lovell and his crew would be marooned hundreds of thousands of miles from Earth.

Lovell was asked, "Were you worried?" Such an obvious question drew snickers. But then Lovell gave a surprising answer.

"No, not really. You see, worry is a useless emotion. I was too busy fixing the problem to worry about it. As long as I had one card left to play, I played it."

That's the secret. Fix the problem, and you won't have time to worry about it. Action is the best antidote to anxiety.

Do something. Tackle whatever it is that's making you anxious. Play your cards.

It was a philosophy that brought three endangered astronauts home from the moon.

It works pretty well here on Earth, too.

Self-Help for Men

**Ginger Rogers did
everything Fred Astaire did—
but she did it backward while
wearing high heels.**

The seminar business is booming these days.

Every time you open a newspaper, somebody's conducting some session for women, aimed at helping them cope:

How to juggle marriage and a career.

How to balance family and job.

How to live on a budget or lose weight.

You have to wonder why so many of these personal self-improvement programs are aimed at women.

I realize women have to do things twice as well as men to be thought half as good, but generally that's not too difficult.

So how about some self-help seminars for men?

One might be called "You Can Do Housework, Too!"

Or how about "Parenting! Participation Does Not End with Conception!"?

A few other helpful seminars for men might include:

"Get a Life—Learn to Cook."

"How *Not* to Act Younger Than Your Children."

"The Remote Control—Overcoming Your Dependence."

Certainly most of us men could use some training in "How to Remember Those Special Occasions."

One morning my wife asked, "Mort, do you know what day this is?"

At that moment I didn't have a clue but figured the best defense was a good bluff. "Of course I do," I snapped back as I hurriedly walked out of the kitchen.

All the way to work I tried to figure it out. It wasn't our anniversary. Not her birthday. Not the day we got engaged.

I couldn't remember.

But it had to be something special for her to mention it. So I sent flowers. I showed up that evening with gift-wrapped earrings and a dinner reservation.

As we headed for the car, I said, "Well, honey, did I remember this day, or didn't I?"

And she said, "You certainly did. This is the best Groundhog Day I've ever had."

"The Glass *Is*"

**Those who think there are only
two sides to every question have a lot
to learn about questions!**

All of our lives we've been conditioned to think in terms of *opposites:*

Up or down.

Black or white.

Big or small.

Fast or slow.

Good or bad.

This simplistic way of dividing life into *equal and opposite* pairings restricts our ability to recognize complexities. Subtleties. Nuances.

Not everything can be so simply understood. Not everything breaks down into easy opposites.

Here's an example. Remember the classic definition of an optimist and a pessimist? An optimist sees the glass of water as half full while the pessimist sees that same glass as half empty. Two views of the same reality. Positive-negative.

But consider how many other views of that same glass are possible:

The realist doesn't deal with the issue of how much water the glass contains. The realist says simply, "The glass *is*."

The idealist comes along and says, "The glass *should* be full."

Then the anarchist declares, "Break the darn glass."

The capitalist suggests, "Let's sell the glass."

The environmentalist proclaims, "Save the water."

The feminist may look at the glass and observe, "My glass seems less full than *his* glass."

Only two sides to every question?

No doubt we could find more answers if we understood just how many sides there are to most questions.

Make the Choice!

**To be happy live each day
as if it were the first day of your
marriage and the last day
of your vacation.**

A fortune-teller looked into her crystal ball and told the young woman, "You'll be poor and unhappy until you're about 45."

The young woman inquired eagerly, "Then what will happen?"

The fortune-teller replied, "By then you'll be used to it."

We don't want unhappiness to become a way of life so that we simply *get used to it.*

Fortunately happiness is a choice, and we humans have the power to choose it.

Most *un*happy people don't realize this. They think they're unhappy because of a bad marriage or a boring job or because they're poor or in ill health.

But if happiness depended upon circumstances, everyone with a good spouse, exciting job, good health and plenty of money *should* be happy. Yet we know that people in such rosy circumstances have committed suicide.

Happiness isn't circumstantial. It's something we cause to happen when we think and act *positively*.

A few years ago when the studio where I worked produced the daily Mike Douglas show, Mike was interviewing an elderly gentleman who was obviously happy.

Mike said to his guest, "You must have some wonderful secret to be so upbeat about life."

The old fellow looked at Mike and said, "No, sir, I don't have any great secret. It's as plain as anything.

"Every day when I get up in the morning, I have two choices. Either to be happy or to be unhappy. I just choose to be happy, and that's all there is to it."

It's a choice we *each* make.

Every day.

Looking Long Enough

**Can we really believe our own eyes?
There may be more there
than we see.**

My stepson, Jeff, sat on the couch, staring at the newspaper.

"I can't figure out how they *see* it," he said.

He was holding one of those three-dimensional puzzles, which, at first, appear to be only a hodgepodge of multicolored dots and brush strokes.

Finally, by holding the picture at one distance and focusing his eyes at another distance, the images popped out in full, three-dimensional depth.

"Amazing," Jeff said as he contemplated his new view of the pattern. "You just have to look at it long enough. Then you literally see things that weren't there before."

How many things in life might become clear to us if we looked long enough. If we changed our focus. Concentrated. But increasing our vision and changing our viewpoint take both determination and patience.

For the most part we rush through life, seeing only what's on the surface. And, like the three-dimensional puzzle at a casual glance, the picture looks flat and sometimes makes no sense. It's only as we *ponder* what's there and look long enough that it takes on a deeper, fuller dimension.

During the Christmas holidays I spent several delightful hours playing with my 17-month-old grandson. Taking a break from the usual hectic pace of Christmas, I sat on the floor, looking for a long time at this child. I studied his face. I watched him as he clutched his toys. I watched him sleep.

What *wonder* this infant inspired as I got to know him better simply by slowing down. Taking my time. Gazing patiently so that I might know and understand this new little person.

Everyone we meet, every situation we encounter, every experience in life is a picture containing fascinating but invisible nuances. How many of them finally float off the page and into our field of vision really is up to us.

What we're willing to see is what will be there.

No more.

No less.

On Public Fascination

Who decides just who becomes a celebrity? You may not like the answer.

"It's a shame you newspeople devote so much time and attention to the criminals," the man complained. "If you wouldn't make celebrities out of them, maybe crime wouldn't seem so glamorous."

He was incensed that people like Charles Manson can write books and grab large chunks of television time for national interviews.

But wait a minute.

Who is it, really, who creates celebrities? Newscasts and newspapers may provide the first exposure, but it's public fascination that keeps a name in the headlines.

It wasn't the publisher who determined that O. J. Simpson's book, written from jail, would become a hot seller. The people who buy books decided that.

Hollywood, too, lives and dies by the bottom line. That's

why there have been three movies about Joey Buttafuoco but not one about Leonardo da Vinci.

In a recent *Times-Mirror* poll only half of us knew Boris Yeltsin was president of Russia. Only 13 percent knew Boutros Boutros Ghali was then secretary general of the U.N.

But 69 percent identified TV producer Aaron Spelling.

A man seemed nervous as he walked into a lawyer's office in Chicago and announced, "I just shot my wife, knifed my boss to death, wiped out my sister's family and raped six women."

"You want to turn yourself in?" the lawyer asked.

"No," the man said. "I'd like you to recommend a publisher. There's no doubt I've got the stuff here for a bestseller!"

Listen!

There's a reason why we were born with two ears but only one mouth!

This answer might not work on a test in anatomy or biology. But it makes sense to me:

We're born with two ears but only one mouth because there's twice as much worth hearing as there is worth saying.

If we listened more and talked less, we'd repair many communication breakdowns.

Breakdowns between wives and husbands.

Between children and parents.

Between workers and bosses.

Patients and doctors.

Friends.

Enemies.

How much we all need to recover the lost art of listening.

The best doctors and nurses understand this. Perhaps that's why I found the following words, unsigned, on a bulletin board in a hospital staff lounge:

When I ask you to listen to me
and you start giving advice,
you have not done what I asked.

When I ask you to listen to me
and you begin to tell me why I shouldn't feel that way,
you are trampling on my feelings.

When I ask you to listen to me
and you feel you have to do something to solve
my problems, you have failed me,
strange as that may seem.

Listen! All I asked was that you listen.
Not talk or do. Just hear me.
Advice is cheap: 25 cents will get you both
Dear Abby and Billy Graham in the same newspaper.
Perhaps that's why prayer works, sometimes,
for some people.
Because God is mute and he doesn't give advice or
try to fix things.
He lets you work it out for yourself.
So please listen and just hear me.
If you want to talk, wait a minute for your turn.

And I'll listen to you.

Trash Collection?

**I call it the careful preservation
of potentially useful materials.
My wife calls it *pack rat* syndrome!**

To her the boxes under my workbench are filled with junk.

I know better. Those boxes contain valuable inventory: unsorted parts for repair jobs that haven't come up yet. But they might.

Forget the fact that when a job does come up, I can never locate the necessary screw, bolt, nail, flange or piece of dowel within that extensive collection. Inevitably I end up at the hardware store, where *their* parts are impressively organized the way mine will be. Someday.

I guess, if truth be told, I am a certified pack rat.

My addiction to saving everything is so serious we recently rented one of those storage units. Now, like our garage and attic, it's filled with stuff that, I tell myself, someday, somebody in our family may want.

Unfortunately this divergence of viewpoint isn't limited to the Crim household. I've concluded that the most serious division in our country today is not between liberals and conservatives.

It's between hoarders and tossers. Pack rats trigger more marital discord than politics.

Renee has come up with a practical solution for us: When anything comes *into* the house, something has to go *out*. (This rule applies to everything except the boxes of parts under my workbench.)

Actually this may be a good policy for all of life—dropping something each time we add something.

Do our calendars become hopelessly cluttered because we take on *new* obligations without getting rid of *old* ones?

Do our emotions become overloaded because we insist on clinging to useless or harmful feelings?

Some things ought to be saved, such as beautiful memories and feelings of love and gratitude. But these can be crowded out if we allow too much trash to collect.

Here's an idea: This weekend, instead of cleaning out the garage, we might spend some time sorting through our minds and emotions and getting rid of the junk we've accumulated over the years. The hurts. The regrets. The anger. The anxieties.

Just a lot of stuff we really don't need to hang on to.

"Grow Up!"

**Whatever happened to accidents?
Where does it say that for every
victim there must be a villain?**

D id Congress outlaw *accidents* when we weren't looking?

Somewhere, somebody must have decided there is no such thing as a mishap without blame.

They've rigged the scales of justice so that for every person who suffers pain, there must be another person who caused it.

Trip on a sidewalk, lose a job, bang your thumb with a hammer, and somebody *has* to be at fault. It couldn't have been just one of those things that happen because our society doesn't believe in accidents anymore.

Now it's easy enough to blame lawyers, anxious to turn your misfortune into their fortune.

But the problem goes beyond money and unscrupulous attorneys. It represents a change in philosophy—a new and naive notion—that *all accidents* are somehow preventable if only we identify causes.

Frequently that means finding the individual or corporation who's responsible. Rarely does it mean examining our own behavior or stupidity to see what role we might have played in creating our own difficulty.

Look at some of the *silly* suits jamming our court dockets:

Is the manufacturer really at fault when the baby stroller tumbles downstairs because some adult wasn't paying attention?

Are carmakers really to blame for all the drunk or careless motorists who drive their products?

There *are* legitimate cases of negligence.

But life is unpredictable, humans are frail and people do make honest mistakes.

There really are *accidents*—inevitable and unpreventable, where nobody is to blame.

It's a mark of maturity to accept that some things in life just happen.

As Joan Rivers might say, "Grow up!"

An Inventory

**The list of things money
can buy is impressive. The list of
things it *can't* is awesome!**

W e didn't have a lot of money when I was growing up.

So it seemed strange to me that my father would always say, "If money can fix it, don't worry about it."

Eventually I came to understand what he meant.

He meant that life's most *serious* losses aren't about *things.* Clothes, jewelry, cars and houses can be replaced or rebuilt.

As a clergyman, Dad had faced, with countless of his parishioners, those somber losses which no amount of money could replace.

Dad knew people who would have given all they owned to have good health restored. To have broken relationships repaired. To have disastrous decisions reversed.

That's why, even though we didn't have much money, Dad could advise us children: *If money can fix it, don't worry about it.*

In a society that equates value and worth with dollars, it's useful sometimes to inventory those things in our lives money *can't* buy.

There are, of course, the obvious: health for ourselves and our families. Satisfaction in our work. Happy marriages.

But there's so much more.

My list would include phone calls from my children living in distant cities.

A letter from my mother.

Cuddling my grandchild.

Reading.

Watching the cat sleep in front of the fire.

Walking our dog through the woods.

Birds on the windowsill announcing spring's arrival.

The breeze off the lake.

Bass fishing.

Music.

These are some of the most valued things in my life.

Come to think of it, the *most* important things aren't *things*.

The Most Important Audience

The first rule for writing a successful screenplay is also the first rule for scripting a successful *life!*

Jim Burnstein is a successful screenwriter.

His script *Renaissance Man,* starring Danny DeVito, had barely hit the big screen when Disney signed him to do another screenplay.

When a young, aspiring writer asked him, "How do you write a script the studios will like?"

Jim Burnstein replied, "Forget the studios. Write for yourself."

He said that too many aspiring writers try to anticipate what certain Hollywood producers might want. Then, instead of writing from their own convictions—their own experiences—they attempt to *customize* a script to the market.

Inevitably they fail because by the time they've completed a script, Hollywood's tastes have changed. They also fail because, in Burnstein's view, "You can't write a good script unless it comes from inside."

Jim's philosophy works in any field. To be successful never play to the crowd. Always play to yourself first.

Live life on the basis of *your* convictions, *your* deepest beliefs—not those you think someone expects.

This means being an original, not an imitation.

The most successful authors I've known—and the most enduring artists and musicians—write or paint or compose from personal experiences. They don't create their work to meet some market they perceive is out there.

Real success in art or in life begins with pleasing that most important audience of all: ourselves.

If we don't, there isn't enough applause in the world to drown out our own ultimate disappointment.

"The Inmates Are Running the Asylum"

For a young mother it's the perfect gift. And it doesn't cost anything.

My friend came home from work to find his wife seated in the middle of the kitchen floor, pots and pans strewn everywhere. Their little boy, a toddler, was banging one of the pans with a wooden spoon. His older sister was running a fire truck across the floor, making siren sounds.

Surveying the scene as he headed for the den, he quipped, "Looks like the inmates are running the asylum."

Actually he's a very devoted and caring husband. That evening they called in the baby-sitter, and he took Mom out for a quiet dinner.

That was nice. But this young mother says it's not the *ultimate* gift. The ultimate gift—the one she cherishes most—is quiet time *alone.*

My friend understands that. So he makes it part of his Saturday routine to take the kids with him on his round of errands.

No matter how much we love our children, constant, unrelieved exposure to their needs by either parent can be extremely stressful.

Some women have figured out ingenious ways to create private time:

I heard of one mom who was playing cops and robbers in the backyard on a summer evening. One of her boys pointed a toy gun and shouted, "Bang, you're dead." She slumped to the ground, and when she didn't get up, a neighbor ran over to see what was wrong.

As the neighbor bent over, Mom opened one eye and whispered, "Shhhh . . . don't blow my cover. It's the only chance I get to rest."

In Hot Water up to Your Nose?

**Some people believe it's problems
that produce stress. It's *not*.**

It was a simple sentence wrapped inside a fortune cookie: *Optimism is a cheerful frame of mind that enables a teakettle to sing though in hot water up to its nose.*

We know about the *hot water* part:

Too many appointments, too little time.

Too many bills, too little money.

A friend of mine returned from a stress workshop and had terrific results. He says it didn't end his stress but now he worries much more effectively.

We tend to think it's the problems in our lives that cause stress. But stress isn't produced by problems. Stress results from how we *react* to problems.

We can't always pick our difficulties. But we can learn to choose our response.

Here's an example: As an instrument-rated pilot I enjoy flying in clouds and having to rely upon the airplane's instruments and my own skills.

I find this kind of challenge exhilarating—not stressful. I've discovered that my nonpilot passengers generally prefer flying in clear skies so that they can see the ground. The instrument conditions, which are fun for me, can be stressful for them.

So stress clearly isn't a condition. It's a response.

Here's another example: My wife Renee finds shopping for clothes a pleasant, exhilarating experience. Frankly I'm much more relaxed flying around in the clouds.

Dr. Elana Tobin says, "Pain is inevitable in life. But suffering is optional."

Maybe we can't avoid sometimes getting into hot water up to our noses.

But it really is *our choice:*

We can boil.

Or we can sing.

The Best Antidote

It isn't *activity* that makes us tired. It's *attitude!*

The doctor's day routinely began at 5:00 A.M. It ended, typically, around seven at night. Sometimes there would be a seminar or a dinner to attend in the evening. Yet he never seemed tired.

"How do you manage such long days without being worn out?" I asked him.

"I guess taking care of myself is part of it," he said. "I jog every morning and try to watch what I eat. But I think the biggest factor is—*I love my work.*"

Enjoyment does energize. Loving their work is one characteristic high-energy people seem to share. Boredom, on the other hand, is exhausting.

I've known entrepreneurs so passionate about their ventures that they could—and would—work sunup to sundown with no apparent signs of fatigue. I've seen other younger workers weary before their day even started.

Work isn't the primary cause of exhaustion. It isn't mental

or physical effort that depletes our energies. It's negative attitudes. Worry. Resentment. Anger. Feelings of not being appreciated. Of being trapped in a job or a relationship.

These attitudes will produce more fatigue than any amount of effort.

Common sense tells us that to be our best and to feel our best, we need rest, exercise and a healthy diet. But beyond those basics the most decisive factor in maintaining energy is enthusiasm. About our work.

About our futures.

About life.

It's the best antidote to tiredness you'll ever find. Don't leave home without it.

"The Tent with the TV Antenna"

**Until a couple has gone camping
together, they don't know how
rough *roughing it* can get!**

Few things reinvigorate a marriage like a weekend of roughing it.

Now understand, *roughing it* doesn't mean the same to a woman as it does to a man.

For Renee *roughing it* is when the motel TV doesn't work.

For me *roughing it* means dueling with nature, pitting my skills against nature and the elements.

So I was less than pleased when Renee pulled a hair dryer and a curling iron out of her knapsack.

"Where," I asked, "do you expect to plug those things in here in the tent?"

"I'm assuming I can use the portable generator you brought for your power tools," she countered.

"Power tools are different," I replied, trying not to sound defensive. "We may have to build a lean-to in case the tent's too small."

"It wouldn't be too small if you hadn't brought your folding desk and word processor," she shot back.

That was a low blow. After all, a writer never knows when inspiration will strike. A writer might leave home without American Express but *never* without a word processor.

"And how about that portable fax machine?" she demanded. The question was unworthy of an answer.

It was at that moment that I saw Renee slip something over behind the portable refrigerator.

It was a portable vacuum cleaner. "If we have to live in a tent," she said, "at least it's going to be clean."

That was it. I was so agitated by all the electric gadgets she'd dragged along that I reached for my cellular phone, made a restaurant reservation and called a cab.

I told him our tent would be easy to find: It was the one with the TV antenna taped to the pole.

Right beside the portable satellite dish.

Say *Yes*

What's the most important quality to look for in a friend?

Choosing friends is serious business.

After all, the people closest to us have a profound influence upon our attitudes, our success and, ultimately, our happiness.

My friends are an odd lot. They're so different in age, background and opinions that you have to wonder whether they have anything in common.

My friends include men and women, some younger, some older than me. They hold all kinds of jobs and all kinds of political views. They represent many religions and no religion.

So what is it that brings such diverse people together into a circle of friendship?

I believe the common denominator is the word *yes*. In one way or another they all say *yes* to life.

In other words my friends are all *positive* people.

They view the dilemmas of life as opportunities and the difficulties of life as challenges to their creativity and skill.

It's easy to develop the habit of saying *no* to new ideas and fresh endeavors.

It's easy to come up with reasons why something won't or shouldn't work. But saying *no* to life isn't productive. People who succeed on the job or at home are people who believe in the possibilities of life. Who proceed as though there just may be an answer to even the toughest problem if they look long enough and work hard enough.

Noted criminal lawyer Clarence Darrow was asked to take part in a debate. He accepted. But when questioned about his familiarity with the subject, Darrow acknowledged he knew very little about it.

"Then how can you possibly debate?" he was asked.

"It's easy," Darrow replied. "I'll just take the negative side. I can argue *against* anything!"

Every scientific and technological advance was accomplished despite critics arguing *against* it or saying it couldn't be done.

We can't stop those who make a habit of saying no.

We can make it a habit to ignore them.

We certainly don't have to make friends of them.

Savoring Each Bite

**Let's test your memory.
Can you remember last week?
Or even yesterday?**

I was browsing through a rack of birthday cards when this line caught my attention:

"We do not remember days, we remember moments."

Think about it.

Can we ever really remember a whole day? Even yesterday?

Not likely. When any nostalgic thought occurs, it's a moment we're recalling.

We may think, *What a terrific vacation that was,* but what we're actually remembering is that instant when our exuberant toddler picked up the shell on the beach. Or the moment we took the hand of someone we loved and shared a sunset.

It's the moments, good and bad, happy and disappointing, which are woven into memory to make up the fabric of our years.

Memories aren't videotapes. They're snapshots. They freeze for us a particular word. Expression. Mood. They

reinflict the sharp pain of a phone call, or rekindle the joy of
a letter or a kiss.

When that little son or daughter asks for a moment of our
time to play or to read or simply to listen, when our coworker
asks for a moment of our time for advice or simply for us to
be there, that child or colleague is actually offering us a valuable opportunity. It's a chance to create memories that will
linger long after the child is grown or the work is completed.

Life becomes richer when we begin to think of it—to experience it—one moment at a time.

Like a superbly prepared meal, *life itself* is enjoyed more
when we savor each bite, relish each distinctive flavor.

Even a Weed . . .

Some of today's junk will be tomorrow's treasures. If only we knew *which junk!*

While studying drama in college, our daughter was required to work on the stage crew.

"It's such a waste of time, Dad," she complained. "I plan to *act,* not build sets."

Shortly after she graduated, Carey directed a play—something she hadn't anticipated doing while in college. When a last-minute repair had to be made on the set, she was able to grab an electric drill and a staple gun and do the job.

In high school I was bored by math. I had no interest in a business or technical career, so for me it seemed a waste of time. Little did I realize that someday I would learn to fly airplanes and eventually go into business—both of which demand mathematical skills. What had seemed like a waste became a necessity.

You know what a Slinky is—that tightly coiled steel spring that walks down stairs. The Slinky started as a scrap on the desk of engineer Richard James. He and his wife, Betty, thought it would make a great toy, and they turned that steel into gold: Slinky, which began life as junk, became a multi-million-dollar success.

Today we may face some boring task or idle conversation that feels like a complete waste of time. Perhaps next week or next year we'll understand that nothing is wasted, that in the economy of our universe even a weed is simply a flower whose use has yet to be discovered.

"I Want It Right Now"

**Marilyn Monroe once described
herself as someone who's been on a
calendar but never on time.**

What *is* our hurry, anyway?

There's a condition that's proved fatal to private pilots, and all of us who fly are familiar with it. We call it *get-home-itis.*

It's that feeling of urgency that overcomes judgment, causing a pilot to believe he really has to get home right now, despite personal fatigue, an underequipped airplane or dangerous weather.

Even when impatience doesn't threaten our lives, it can be costly. An orthopedic surgeon I know says many of his patients could avoid surgery if only they were willing to wait. He says time and physical therapy often would do the job. But never as quickly as surgery. So, many patients opt for the knife rather than waiting for natural healing.

Our culture conditions us to think impulsively and to expect instant answers.

Pictures are developed in an hour.

Oil is changed in 10 minutes.

We drive through for hamburgers—and cash—without leaving our cars.

One TV commercial for a dance studio promises, "Walk in, dance out."

A colleague has this prayer posted above her desk: "God grant me patience, and I want it right now."

Why do we insist on treating life as some pill to be quickly swallowed?

Shouldn't it be a gourmet meal that we leisurely savor and enjoy?

Only when we learn to slow down and take life as it comes can we truly draw both the beauty and the pleasure from each moment.

We Have the Choice

**What is the *one thing*
we humans can do that no
other creature can?**

When it comes to competing with the animals, I'm afraid we humans will lose almost every time. I say *almost* because there is one notable exception.

We'll never win in the strength or speed departments:

My son once had a Doberman that could easily outrun me.

The squirrels in our yard can jump farther and balance better than I can.

One of my wife's favorite beach activities is watching pelicans fly by in precise formation. No human aviators ever flew more gracefully.

Clearly there are creatures that can outrun the fastest Olympic athlete, outmaneuver the most skilled mountain climber and outfly the most highly trained human pilot.

But there is one quality that is unique to the human species:

We have the ability to be noble.

To put another's interest above our own.

To act *heroically.* To give our time, our money and even our lives for someone or some cause.

In a word, we humans—and we alone—are capable of *commitment.*

The soldier who throws himself on top of a grenade to save a buddy; the mother who sacrifices a kidney so that her dying child can live; the firefighter who risks his own life to pull someone he's never met, unconscious, from a burning building—these acts of heroism are a choice, and it's a choice only humans can make.

Yes, we have seen animals forfeit their lives for their young. We've heard of pets risking their own lives for an owner. But these are instinctive reactions, not the result of rational decisions to sacrifice. Only people possess this capability.

The ability to deny ourselves, to choose altruism over selfishness, heroism over self-preservation—this defines our humanity.

We humans may not always act heroically.

But we do have the choice.

"Not Another Thing"

**If you could be any
age you wanted, what age
would it be?**

Dad was in his late 50s when I asked him, "What was your favorite age?"

Without a moment's hesitation, he replied, "This age. I like right where I am. Wouldn't want to go back."

In his 60s, Dad felt exactly the same way.

As I grow older, I'm starting to understand that attitude, which, frankly, made little sense to me at the time.

Wouldn't people prefer to stay in their 20s or 30s, with all the vigor and enthusiasm, all the potential and opportunity that naturally accompany youth?

Surely most people would at least want to stop the clock in their 40s if they could.

But, like my father, those who live well and wisely discover that each age—each decade—brings its own rewards, its own satisfactions.

It's always comforting to encounter older people who believe their present stage in life is the best, since all of us are heading in their direction.

To meet a senior citizen who's enjoying the freedom of retirement, the pleasure of grandparenting, the fun of pursuing hobbies or even a second or third career—this gives hope to the rest of us.

. Of course it's natural to occasionally long for the extra energy and boundless enthusiasm we recall from our teen years. In Minneapolis, Jimmy Caruthers's mom must have been thinking along those lines when he asked her advice about a birthday gift for his girlfriend.

"If you were going to be 16 years old tomorrow, what would *you* want?" he inquired.

And with no hesitation his mother replied, "Not another thing, Jimmy. Not another thing."

Furnishing Your Mind

**One of your most valuable
possessions can never be
taken from you.**

Someone could steal your car or your stereo.

Someone could break into your house and clean out all your valuable possessions.

Yet you and I possess something of unspeakable value that can never be stolen.

It's our *imagination.*

How valuable?

A former prisoner of war told me how imagination had preserved his sanity while he was confined in a small concrete cell in North Vietnam. For three years he would imagine himself at home with family and friends or outside sitting under a tree, reading.

At times he'd write stories in his mind, then read to himself from his imaginary book.

During the final months of my father's life, when he was confined to bed, Dad would talk about how he had "furnished his mind" with so many good things—things he could now draw upon. Without ever leaving his room, Dad could revisit places and review events that would have been denied to him without his fertile and active imagination.

One of the most amazing stories about the power of imagination comes from China, where Liu Shih-kum was a world-renowned concert pianist at age 19. He placed second in the International Tchaikovsky competition.

Then came Mao Tse-tung's bloody purge—the so-called Cultural Revolution—and Liu was thrown into prison for refusing to denounce Western music.

He was brutalized, and during one beating his arm was badly broken.

After six years in confinement with no books, no music and no piano, Liu was summoned for propaganda purposes to appear with the visiting Philadelphia Orchestra.

He not only performed, he played brilliantly.

How could this have happened?

Liu explained: During those six years in prison he'd created a piano in his mind and practiced it faithfully every day. That imaginary piano was one his guards couldn't see, couldn't hear and couldn't take away.

An imagination is a terrible thing to waste.

The Fuel of Life

**The greatest gift in the world
is something we can *all*
give our children!**

If you could leave a single gift to your children, what would you choose?

Wealth?

Knowledge?

Talent?

Intellect?

If I could leave only *one* gift, it would be *enthusiasm.*

So many of the other good things in life depend upon it.

How important is wealth if life is a bore?

What good is knowledge if life is without meaning?

Talent and intelligence don't count for much if we are apathetic about life itself.

Enthusiasm can *generate* wealth.

It can motivate us to *pursue* knowledge. Enthusiasm may provide the spark that enhances talent, inspires intellect and propels us toward personal and professional success.

Enthusiasm can even help regenerate health.

I would rather bequeath my children enthusiasm than money or talent because the world has its share of miserable millionaires and able people whose ability remains undeveloped because they don't really care.

How many people can we count who have outperformed their own talent or outpaced their own intelligence simply by being *enthusiastic?*

As a pilot I like to fly airplanes that are well equipped with sophisticated instruments. Planes that are well maintained. But the most expensive, most well equipped airplane in the world won't run very far without fuel.

Enthusiasm is the *fuel of life.* It's what propels us all, rich and poor, healthy and sick, famous and obscure.

If I could leave my children only one gift, it would be enthusiasm.

With enthusiasm, they might acquire the other good things in life.

Without enthusiasm, how much would the rest really matter?

Wealthy—Or Rich?

The only difference between men and boys is the amount of money they spend on their toys!

Most people would agree: It's important to get what we want.

But it's probably more important to want what we get.

And that may be even more difficult.

Star Trek's Mr. Spock has made some rather down-to-earth observations. He once said: "After a time, you may find that having is not so pleasant a thing after all as wanting. It is not logical, but it is often true."

Driving past the private hangar at our local airport, my friend took quick inventory. There was a beautifully restored aerobatic biplane; behind that, a larger, twin-engine passenger plane; and next to that, an antique classic sports car. There were also two motorcycles and a very nice boat on a trailer.

"Well, he's certainly got all the toys," my friend said. That made me think of the bumper sticker that says: *He who dies with the most toys, wins.*

But what does it mean to win?

One of the *richest* people I've ever known died a few years ago, and, frankly, she didn't leave many toys. No airplanes. No boats. No sports cars. Her home was quite modest.

The closest thing she had to toys were some small mementos brought back from Kenya, where she'd devoted 20 years of her life to being a medical missionary.

Perhaps you could count as *toys* the photographs she prized—the ones showing newborn infants she had just delivered. Or village children she had vaccinated. These certainly were among her valued possessions, more important to her than any mere yacht.

Then there were the boxes of letters we found—letters of gratitude from college students whose lives she had touched as campus nurse and substitute mom.

Yes, I guess you'd have to say that when we finished sorting out Aunt Vera's possessions, it was clear she didn't have a lot of toys.

What she did have was a life that was real.

A life that was fulfilled.

One that had purpose. And meaning. And was filled with fun.

Above all, Aunt Vera was happy. One of the happiest people I've ever known. That's why I said she was *rich!* I never said she was wealthy.

Sure makes you wonder. Maybe the person who dies with the most toys *isn't* the one who wins.

In the long run.

Contrails

Nobody slips quietly through life unnoticed. We all leave tracks in the snow.

My uncle Alvah was a rabbit hunter. He loved to hunt in the winter when he could spot rabbit tracks in the snow. Deer hunters look for the same clues.

But rabbit and deer aren't the only creatures that leave evidence of where they've been.

We all do. Like animals leaving snowy imprints in the woods or airplanes streaming puffy contrails through the sky, we humans inevitably *document* our own pathways through life.

Sometimes the trails we leave are inspiring.

Sometimes depressing.

Some of us bring happiness into a room just by entering it. Some by leaving it.

But for better or worse, we are noticed.

I have a friend who leaves a vibrant trail of enthusiasm and hope wherever he goes. He's so upbeat and optimistic that people inevitably feel better when he's been around. For hours after he leaves a place the mood is noticeably more positive.

A woman I know always leaves trails of kindness. A simple word, a small gift, an encouraging touch, a cheerful smile. Her tracks remain long after she's gone.

Of course some people leave dark and gloomy trails of pessimism and bitterness. Of selfishness, criticism and hate.

Flying in my plane along the shore of Lake Erie one afternoon, I saw above me three splendid white contrails shooting from a formation of fighter jets. A few hundred feet below, a long ribbon of brown smoke snaked ominously from a factory stack.

The contrails were inspiring. Something of beauty.

The smoke trail was depressing.

Which kind of trail you and I leave behind is completely a matter of choice.

About the Author

M ort Crim is the creator and voice of the award-winning radio series *Second Thoughts,* airing on more than 700 radio stations worldwide. The 90-second motivational essays reflect Crim's belief that the world needs a break from the violent and the weird exploited in much mainstream news media. He inspires with humor and personal anecdotes in his *Second Thoughts* program, emphasizing his belief in the positive aspects of human nature.

Crim draws on his knowledge of the human condition gained from 30 years of broadcasting experience. He witnessed the Newark riots and the funeral of Robert Kennedy. He was in Vietnam with President Lyndon Johnson and at Cape Canaveral for most of the Apollo moon voyages. He covered the Yom Kippur War in the Middle East. Crim has been on the spot and in the line of fire, reporting major events from Russia, Poland, Germany, Italy and Latin America.

The inspiration inherent in *Second Thoughts* comes easily to Crim who is in demand as a motivational speaker across America on college campuses and at seminars, business forums and conventions.

The son of a minister, he once considered becoming a military chaplain. Instead, he became a journalist, a profession that, he believes, shares many of the values of ministers and teachers.

"We're all in the business of trying to make the world better through enlightenment," he says.

Second Thoughts is not Crim's first venture into uplifting human interest radio. In the 1970s, he created a nationally syndicated series, *One Moment Please,* which aired on more than 350 radio stations. This highly successful series was a blend of philosophy, psychology and personal experience fused into Crim's own unique essay style.

He has been a broadcaster for stations from California to New York City and for five years was a national correspondent for ABC. His was the voice that described Neil Armstrong's landing on the moon for the national ABC radio audience.

Crim was the permanent vacation substitute for Paul Harvey from 1980 to 1984 and was heard several weeks each year on more than 1,300 radio stations.

He is the author of three books: *One Moment Please,* a collection of his radio scripts; *Like It Is,* a journalist's view of how personal convictions apply to everyday life and to the major issues of the day; and his most recent, *Second Thoughts.*

Crim was senior editor and anchor of the evening news at WDIV-TV in Detroit from 1978 to 1997 and continues to serve as WDIV's vice president, community affairs. He has been outspoken on the need to elevate television news from the sensational to the truly significant. He believes networks should give more airtime to human achievement and heroism to balance the reports of human failures and tragedy. United

Press International has twice named his evening newscasts Best Local TV Newscast in America.

Crim serves on the board of directors of the Karmanos Cancer Institute, Alma College, the Coalition of Christian Colleges and Universities, Junior Achievement, the Michigan Thanksgiving Day Parade, Operation ABLE and is on the board of governors for the Detroit Renaissance Club. He is a member of the General Aviation Committee that advises the Michigan Aeronautics Commission on matters of importance to private and corporate aviation. He also serves on advisory boards or committees for the Henry Ford Estate, Hospice of Southeastern Michigan and Michigan Communities in Action for Drug Free Youth.

Crim is a graduate of the University of Nebraska at Omaha and received his Master's degree in Journalism from Northwestern University's Medill School of Journalism. He has received scores of awards including more than a dozen Emmys, Northwestern University's prestigious Alumni Merit Award (School of Journalism) in 1992, Northwestern's Harrington Award for Outstanding Promise in the Field of Journalism and UNO's Distinguished Alumni Achievement Award in 1983. In 1997 he was among the first distinguished Northwestern alumni inducted into Medill's Hall of Achievement.

In 1995 he was awarded the Gold World Medal as Best Radio Personality at the New York Festival's International Radio Awards and the following year received the Festival's Silver Medal for Best Humor Writing.

Besides his very active professional career, Mr. Crim also is a successful entrepreneur who has founded two production companies. He is currently CEO of Mort Crim

Communications, Inc. A licensed commercial pilot, he flies his twin-engine plane to cover news assignments and meet tight business and speaking schedules.

Crim is married to the former Irene (Renee) Bowman Miller. They reside in Saint Clair Shores, Michigan and Ponte Vedra Beach, Florida.

To contact Mort Crim, write or call:

Mort Crim
Mort Crim Communications, Inc.
20416 Harper Avenue
Harperwood, MI 48225
phone (313) 882-4700
fax (313) 882-7414

"Mort Crim is positive, but he's no Pollyanna. In a world of both challenges and opportunities, *Second Thoughts* inspires us to take responsibility and make positive choices."

Steve Bell
chairman, Department of Telecommunications, Ball State University,
and former ABC news correspondent

"A timely and thoughtful reflection on so many of life's trials and tribulations. Mort captures them with warmth, humor and real compassion."

Carmen Harlan
news anchor, WDIV (NBC), Detroit

"Reading Mort's book is like working your way through a crisis and landing successfully on your feet!"

"This collection of 100 remarkable essays, each requiring just 90 seconds of your time, is written by a sensitive and noted broadcaster. It provides insight into everyday life in a positive, uplifting and delightful style. They make for a better outlook on life."

"Mort Crim, congratulations, treasured friend, on your expanding horizons. You are an encourager to an enormous audience, including Paul Harvey."

"This collection of *Second Thoughts* by Mort Crim—whose career in journalism couldn't callous his instinct to see the best in us while reporting the worst—provides a second chance to reflect on his inspiring radio commentaries that have offered a few gentle seconds of wise perspective on a world that badly needs it."

"Mort's everlasting positive outlook on life is always refreshing and inspiring. *Second Thoughts* motivates me in my everyday life. It lifts my spirits!"